Copyright © 2020 Hillsong International Ltd atf Hillsong International

Version 4

Shine program 'Young & Gorgeous'
Reprinted in ©2000 CityCare Ltd
Reprinted in ©2003, ©2005, ©2007, ©2009 as ShineGIRL Hillsong CityCare
Reprinted in ©2012 by Hillsong Church Ltd.

All rights reserved. No part of this book may be reproduced in any form by any mechanical or electronic means including information storage or retrieval systems, without permission in writing from the publisher.

While the manual is consistent with the values of Hillsong, the program and manual are suitable for use within any value or faith-based system. The purpose of this community development program is to promote a holistic, humanitarian and strengths-based approach to life.

Enquiries should be addressed to the publishers.

Hillsong Music Australia, PO Box 1195, Castle Hill NSW 1765, Australia

T: +61 2 8853 5300
F: +61 2 8846 4625
E: resources@hillsong.com

WARNING:

The ShineGIRL Facilitator Handbook and ShineGIRL Journals are provided to help facilitate the running of the ShineGIRL program. Although the content of the program is copyright protected it does NOT constitute, or contain legal, medical or other advice. Use of this handbook and running the program is entirely at your own risk.

Before running this program, you should obtain your own legal, insurance and other professional advice in the State, Territory or Country in which you intend to run the program.

SHINEGIRL FACILITATOR HANDBOOK

ACKNOWLEDGEMENTS SIX
INTRODUCTION SEVEN
SHINEGIRL OVERVIEW EIGHT
PROGRAM INFORMATION ELEVEN
SESSION OUTCOMES THIRTY-ONE
SESSION PLANS THIRTY-FIVE
FOUNDATIONAL CONCEPT 1: WORTH THIRTY-NINE
SESSION ONE: I AM VALUABLE FORTY-SEVEN
SESSION TWO: I AM ONE OF A KIND FIFTY-SEVEN
SESSION THREE: I AM WONDERFULLY MADE SIXTY-SEVEN
FOUNDATIONAL CONCEPT 2: STRENGTH SEVENTY-NINE
SESSION FOUR: I HAVE THE POWER OF CHOICE EIGHTY-FIVE
SESSION FIVE: MY DECISIONS DETERMINE MY DESTINATION NINETY-SEVEN
SESSION SIX: I HAVE RESILIENCE ONE HUNDRED AND THIRTEEN
FOUNDATIONAL CONCEPT 3: PURPOSE ONE HUNDRED AND TWENTY-ONE
SESSION SEVEN: MY POTENTIAL IS LIMITLESS ONE HUNDRED AND TWENTY-SEVEN
SESSION EIGHT: MY LIFE HAS PURPOSE ONE HUNDRED AND THIRTY-SEVEN
SESSION NINE: SHINE! ONE HUNDRED AND FORTY-NINE
APPENDICES ONE HUNDRED AND FIFTY-SIX

acknowledgements.

We would like to acknowledge and thank the following contributors:

DR NANDILLA SPRY DBA, MSD, BA, CERT IV TAE

RENEE YAM M. SEXUAL HEALTH, PGDIPSOCHLTH, CERT IV TAA, B. EC.

SARAH MCMAHON BA (PSYCH), PG DIP (PSYCH), PG DIP (PSYCH PR) ASSOC MAPS

LYDIA JADE TURNER BA (PSYCH) PG DIP (PSYCH) ASSOC MAPS

JO WHITE R.N. CERT IV, AOD, CERT IV TAA

LESLEY SHIELDS CERT IV IN SOCIAL WELFARE, CERT III IN COUNSELLING

WE WOULD LIKE TO THANK **VERA COLEMAN** FOR MAKING IT POSSIBLE TO START THIS JOURNEY IN 1997. THE ULTIMATE TEST OF AN IDEA IS WHETHER IT OUTLIVES US. CHANGING THE WORLD IS A COLLABORATIVE EFFORT. HER COMMITMENT CREATED MANY OPPORTUNITIES FOR WOMEN AND GIRLS ALL OVER THE WORLD TO FLOURISH.

introduction.

The ShineGIRL program is an option for schools and teachers to demonstrate their commitment to the Quality Teaching Framework, School Leadership Capability Framework and Values Education Policy. Additionally, this welfare-based program addresses syllabus outcomes from key learning areas such as from the Personal Development Health and Physical Education (PDHPE) curriculum, along with fostering literacy skills. The structure of ShineGIRL enables schools and teachers to differentiate the content based on the individual learning needs of the participating students and can also be modified for the Life Skills curriculum or individual learning plans.

ShineGIRL is about equipping girls with the knowledge and skills to discover who they are and the person they want to become. It also hopes to offer girls new, proactive positions to co-construct stories of identity in which they discover a new language to speak about what they value and treasure in their lives, and to state their hopes and preferences. As many young people in our communities do not know or believe they are valuable and unique individuals, most struggle to find acceptance amongst their peers and genuine meaning for their life. A common mindset amongst young people is that 'If I am not of much value, then life doesn't have much purpose'. This inevitably creates a sense of 'living for the moment' with little regard for consequences or the future. The impact of this 'meaninglessness of life' and loss of hope is made apparent by the fact that the youth suicide rate continues to increase not just in Australia but worldwide.[1] Lack of purpose instils negative mindsets in the lives of youth and can subsequently control the way they perceive their future. The break-up of the family unit, concerns of body image, coping with stress and young people believing they have little worth or nothing to contribute have far reaching implications – both immediate and long-term.[2]

This program encourages participants to find the strength and courage within themselves to make healthy choices and live to their full potential. The program is not aimed at stereotyping what girls should be like or how they should behave, but using a holistic approach, it reinforces that every girl is different and has different strengths, qualities and skills. Sharing knowledge to open conversations about the uniqueness of each person is a direct affront to the dominant ideas of what makes one beautiful. These ideas subjugate young girls and contribute to non-agentive positions by which young girls grade their worth and value.

Note: This Facilitator Guide and accompanying Journals are provided to help facilitate the running of the Shine program. Although the content of the program is copyright protected it does NOT constitute, or contain legal, medical or other advice. Use of this handbook and running the program, is entirely at your own risk. 1 World Health Organisation (2011). Suicide prevention (SUPRE) Mental Health. [Online] Available: http://www.who.int/mental_health/prevention/suicide/suicideprevent/en/ [14/03/11] 2 Mission Australia (2010) National Survey of Young Australians 2010 © Mission Australia [Online} Available: www.missionaustralia.com.au/downloads/214-national-survey-of-young-australians [14/03/2011]

overview.

ShineGIRL is a unique personal development and group mentoring tool that uses an inspirational, practical and experiential approach to learning. This program is founded upon the premise that every life counts and has intrinsic value, and fosters an awareness of this belief. As a result, girls are equipped to become effective global citizens for the future.

aim.

For each girl to develop understanding of her own personal worth, strength and purpose and realise the potential within her to fulfil her desires.

objectives.

Equip girls to:
Identify themselves as valuable with much to contribute to society.
Build confidence and gain an understanding of intrinsic value.
Develop decision-making and problem-solving skills.
Understand they are able to have a positive influence in their world.
Identify personal desires and strengths to motivate them to set and achieve personal goals.

three foundational concepts: worth. strength. purpose.

i have WORTH!

'BODY AND SOUL, I AM WONDERFULLY MADE'

The focus for these session is for girls to understand for themselves that they are valuable. Their uniqueness is something to celebrate and that they have been wonderfully made.

i have STRENGTH!

'CHOOSE LIFE'

These sessions explore the power of choice and the power that decisions have on shaping a person's future. This is addressed through practical sessions about feelings, convictions, decision-making and problem-solving.

i have PURPOSE!

'I HAVE A HOPE AND A FUTURE'

Purpose is examined through exploring personal hopes, dreams and desires. Goal setting, group discussions on potential talents and practical activities, are used to equip and build confidence to live out a purpose-filled, adventurous life.

SHINEGIRL

PI
program information.

key outcomes.

Girls have achieved learning and motivational outcomes that form the foundation of the ultimate goal – a greater level of understanding about their own personal worth, strength and purpose. These include:

- Developed holistic personal and problem-solving skills
- Improved confidence and understanding of value
- Enhanced social support networks
- Greater understanding in relation to gifts and talents
- Greater awareness of community contribution and participation.

target group.

ShineGIRL is an adaptable course used in various local settings to reach adolescent girls in middle school from Grade 7 to Grade 10. The course can be run in high schools, youth groups, youth centres, residential centres, juvenile detention centres and so forth. This program is not intended to replace the provision of formal case management, counselling or support for children and young people requiring professional assistance or intervention.

approach.

ShineGIRL is characterised by the following:

- 15 participants is the maximum number for a group
- An informal environment to explore the ShineGIRL concepts
- 'Hands-on' practical and interactive sessions
- Group discussions and short teaching sessions (maximum 10 minutes)
- A significant celebration
- Personal stories
- Elements of surprise
- 1 facilitator, 2-3 co-facilitators.

Team Roles

Below are team roles that can be established for your program group. A minimum requirement to run a ShineGIRL program is to have a Lead Facilitator.

Facilitators

LEAD FACILITATOR

The Lead Facilitator is responsible to lead and implement the ShineGIRL program for a group of participants. The Lead Facilitator may or may not have a team working with them.

CO-FACILITATOR(S)

The Co-Facilitator(s) support the Lead Facilitator in running the program. Additional responsibilities include:

- Facilitating activities under the supervision of the Lead Facilitator.
- Having responsibility for a small group of participants within the larger program group e.g. leading the small group discussion segment of a session.

Support Persons

SPECIALIST SUPPORT PERSON

The Specialist Support Person comes alongside the facilitators and works specifically with participants who require extra care and assistance e.g. the School Counsellor.

The Specialist Support Person differs from the Co-Facilitator as they are working in the program with the purpose of assisting specific participants in the program group.

ASSISTANTS

Assistants give practical support to the facilitator(s). Assistants do not facilitate activities or lead small discussion groups. Assistant roles include:

- Set-up and room organisation.
- Helping set out the activity materials throughout the session.
- Assisting the participants practically (under the guidance of a facilitator) e.g. helping find a glue stick, and
- Clean-up.

Examples of an assistant include parent(s)/carer(s) and adult community volunteers.

RESOURCE CO-ORDINATOR

It can be very helpful for a ShineGIRL program group to have a Resource Co-ordinator who can collect and put together the resources needed for each session. This role requires creativity and organisation. Having a Resource Co-ordinator is especially helpful when several ShineGIRL programs are being run by an organisation. They can arrange for resources to be organised and/or purchased in bulk. A Resource Co-ordinator may also manage a team who assist the program groups with their resource requirements.

JUNIOR ASSISTANTS

Junior assistants fulfil the role of an assistant (as outlined above). An example of a Junior Assistant is a Peer Support Leader from the school where the ShineGIRL program is being run. Junior assistants are to come under the definition of children and young people (refer to Child Well-Being and Safety, pp.15-25).

Child Well-Being & Safety

Child Protection Legislation

ORGANISATIONS ARE REQUIRED TO MEET LEGISLATIVE OBLIGATIONS IN RELATION TO CHILD PROTECTION. THEY ARE REQUIRED TO HAVE A CHILD PROTECTION POLICY THAT IS APPLICABLE TO THEIR COUNTRY, STATE OR TERRITORY.

Child protection legislation has been enacted by every state and territory of Australia. This legislation sets out legal and regulatory requirements around the interaction with children and young people, the care of children and young people, and the reporting of conduct of concern.

Facilitators and support persons are to be familiar with the organisation's policies and procedures that:

a) Guide staff and volunteers (i.e. facilitators and support persons) on how to relate to children and young people (i.e. participants and junior assistants).

b) Clarify the parameters of appropriate and inappropriate conduct for staff and volunteers (i.e. facilitators and support persons) to create a safe and supportive environment for the children and young people (i.e. participants and junior assistants).

c) Model a workplace that is collaborative, consultative and lawfully compliant in relation to current child protection practice.
d) Outline procedures for training and practice for staff and volunteers (i.e. facilitators and support persons) to fulfil their responsibilities:
   i) Under the specifications of legislation in terms of having a valid Working with Children's Check (WWCC[1]) (or equivalent standards of the country, state or territory where the ShineGIRL program is run) and appropriate conduct.
   ii) To report inappropriate conduct directed towards children and young people.
   iii) As Mandatory Reporters of concerns for children and young people at risk of significant harm.

---

[1] In New South Wales, Australia, before engaging a new, paid or volunteer, child-related worker, an organisation must ensure the worker has a clearance to work with children. The only way for an organisation to determine a person's clearance status is by verifying their WWCC with The Office of the Guardian.

Child Well-Being Coordinator

Organisations should designate a lead Child Well-Being Coordinator who is aware of all the ShineGIRL programs that are occurring within their organisation. This person must be knowledgeable and experienced with child protection legislation for children and young people under the age of 18. They must be willing to be the key point of contact for all facilitators and support persons who will be involved in working with the children and young people participating in the ShineGIRL program.

The Child Well-Being Coordinator must know the Child Well-Being requirements for their country, state or territory. They must prepare both the facilitators and support persons before each program is run and respond if there are concerns regarding child well-being and safety. In short, the coordinator must prevent and respond by:

- Coordinating processes to ensure all selected facilitators and support persons are safe and trusted adults.
    - Verify and record the status of the their WWCC (or equivalent standards of the country, state or territory where the ShineGIRL program is run), and
    - Only engage child-related workers or eligible volunteers who have a valid WWCC.
    - Report findings of misconduct involving children and young people made against child-related workers or volunteers, and
    - Complete reference checks for facilitators and support persons.
- Ensure that the facilitators and support persons involved in the program have appropriate training.
- If there are concerns during the course of the program, implement policy and specific procedures e.g. identify, respond to and support children and young people when there are child well-being and safety risks and/or concerns.

Duty of Care

All facilitators and support persons have a duty to take reasonable care for the safety and welfare of the children and young people (i.e. participants and junior assistants) in their care.

This duty is to consider and take all reasonable action to protect children and young people (i.e. participants and junior assistants) from known hazards or risk of harm that can be reasonably predicted. The standard of care that is required by a facilitator or a support person must take into consideration various factors, such as a child or young person's maturity and ability.

The duty of care responsibility for children and young people (i.e. participants and junior assistants) exercised by all facilitators and support persons applies during all activities and functions conducted or arranged by the organisation where a child or young person is in the care of facilitators and support persons.

The risk associated with any activity needs to be assessed and managed by facilitators and support persons before the activity is undertaken. A single serious failure to exercise appropriate duty of care, or persistent repeated failures, may constitute neglect or negligence according to the law if significant harm is caused or if there is the potential to cause significant harm to a child or young person (i.e. participant or junior assistant).

Permissions

Before a child or young person (i.e. participant or junior assistant) engages in the ShineGIRL program, consent to participate is to be obtained from parent(s)/guardian(s) and/or the hosting organisation's contact person who is responsible for the children and young people e.g. in a school, it is the Principal.

Where a child or young person (i.e. participant or junior assistant) leaves the premises for an excursion (e.g. movie) or outing (e.g. going to a local sports oval to run a session activity), a permission slip for each child and young person is required to be signed by their parent/guardian. Where the program is run at a school, excursions or outings:

- Must first be approved by the school e.g. by the Principal.
- Permission slips are to be organised by the school contact, and
- Can only be run if a school staff member attends and has primary responsibility for the children.

Professional Relations with Participants

All facilitators and support persons are to be caring and supportive adults who take an interest in the well-being of young people (i.e. participants and junior assistants), and who set appropriate boundaries for relations with children.

At all times, facilitators and support persons must treat children and young people (i.e. participants and junior assistants) with respect and behave in ways that promote their safety, welfare and well-being. Facilitators and support persons are always to act professionally. Your organisation's policies (that comply with the country state or territory's legislation where the ShineGIRL program is run) will outline ways to assist facilitators and support persons maintain a correct professional relationship and boundaries with children and young people.

Where a small gift is provided to the participants during a session, the gift needs to be similar for each participant in the program group but may be customised for the individual e.g. if participants are each given a wooden alphabet letter the gift would customised by providing each participant with the letter of their first name or preferred name. There can be no differentiation in the quality or type of the gift as this can be viewed as favouritism.

Where a small gift is provided to each junior assistant to appreciate their time and contribution to the program group, the gift needs to be similar for each junior assistant but can be customised for the individual. The gift should be given on behalf of the ShineGIRL program Group to the Junior Assistant. A good time to do this is in the last session.

Confidentiality

It is important that all facilitators and support persons are aware of their confidentiality requirements. This means that discussions with community members about specific program groups or individuals are not allowed. Likewise, posting photos or comments about specific program groups or individuals on the Internet e.g. websites and social media, without consent is prohibited. Do not allow participants to take photographic or audio-visual material during the session.

Confidentiality does **NOT** extend to areas including:

- Mandatory reporting under child protection legislation. In a school in NSW Australia, mandatory reporting concerns must go directly to the principal and are not to be discussed with others e.g. team members, the classroom teacher or parent(s)/guardian(s). This will be outlined in the school's policies, however, this does not relieve the facilitator or support person from their obligation to be a mandatory reporter. For example, the seriousness of an allegation may warrant immediate contact with the police.
- When there is a serious threat to the life, health or safety to a person(s).
- Where program groups and/or individuals are discussed in the appropriate context e.g. communicating with your team, a child's parent/guardian or specific school staff about non-mandatory reporting issues.
- Where a signed and authorised use of image form is provided by the parent/guardian for audio visual, written or photographic material to be used from the participants e.g. on the organisation's promotional material, website or social media platform. Note: this is only applicable if it is compliant to the organisations policy e.g. a school may not permit photos to be taken at school events.

Practical Guidelines

Please note these are guidelines only. Team members are to follow their organisation's Child Well-Being and Safety policies that comply with their country and state or territory's legislation.

Please select one of the following applicable to your ShineGIRL program group and read the corresponding information.

1. Facilitating the program at your venue, or
2. Facilitating the program where another organisation is hosting.

1. Facilitating the Program at Your Venue

COMMUNICATION WITH TEAM MEMBERS

- Identification must be worn by facilitators and support persons.
- Ensure facilitators and support persons have access to a phone in case of emergency.
- Team members are not to be alone with children and young people (i.e. participants and junior assistants) where they cannot be seen by others. Keep areas open with team members visible. For example, do not shut blinds or curtains in this situation.
- Do not initiate physical contact with children or young people (i.e. participants and junior assistants). When responding to appropriate physical contact initiated by younger participants, a shoulder hug, a pat on the back or a hand-hold are the only appropriate responses.
- Facilitators are to plan activities and responses are to be anticipated. If the participants become increasingly difficult to manage during an activity the Lead Facilitator is to stop the activity and regain management of the situation e.g. stop the activity and have the participants return to their desks.
- The Lead Facilitator is to have a key contact person's details who is available in case of emergency or where an immediate concern is identified e.g. a welfare officer. In a school in NSW Australia, if a reportable or potential reportable child protection matter arises, a person is required to tell the principal directly.
- Ensure the Lead Facilitator has the contact number(s) for each child and young person's (i.e. participants and junior assistants) parent(s)/guardian(s) and that these are kept current. It is advisable to have a secondary contact for each child and young person for use in case of emergency e.g. where the primary contact cannot be reached.
- Facilitators and support persons are to be fully aware of the venue protocols including:
    - Evacuation and lock down procedures.
    - First aid procedures, and
    - Location of bathrooms.
- Debrief with the team after each session e.g. What worked well? What can be improved? Are there any concerns about a child or young person? Are there any concerns about the venue? It is important concerns are documented and referrals made where needed.

COMMUNICATION WITH CHILDREN AND YOUNG PEOPLE
- Junior assistants are to come under the definition of children and young people.
- Children and young people (i.e. participants and junior assistants) are to go to bathrooms and/or other enclosed areas in groups and are not to go alone. Adult team members are not to be in the bathroom at the same time as children and young people.
- Children and young people (i.e. participants and junior assistants) need to be able to describe procedures for arriving and departing each session e.g. once their parent/guardian leaves them at the program they are to remain in the program until their parent/guardian returns and they are signed-out of the session.

COMMUNICATION WITH PARENT(S)/GUARDIAN(S)
- Intentionally communicate with parent(s)/guardian(s) about the program and their child's participation e.g. an information session, emails, SMS, posters/signs. Build relationships that are strong, positive and helpful.
- Determine a registration and dismissal process for the program. All children and young people (participants and junior assistants) should be signed in and out of each session.
- Communicate clearly and openly with parent(s)/guardian(s) around logistics for their child (i.e. participant or student volunteer) including the drop-off and pick-up time and location. Have a clear process for what happens if a:
  - Parent/guardian is late to collect their child.
  - Third-party will be collecting a child or young person from the program e.g. a family friend, or
  - A child is making their own way to and/or from the program e.g. using public transport.

NOTE ON FACILITATING THE PROGRAM AT YOUR VENUE:
Where the venue is a school and the Lead Facilitator is a school staff member e.g. a teacher, the person will already be aware of the school's policies and is to simply run the program within that framework.

2. Facilitating The Program Where Another Organisation Is Hosting

For a program being run in partnership with a hosting organisation, the guidelines below should be discussed e.g. with the key contact person in a school.

COMMUNICATION WITH TEAM MEMBERS:
- Identification must be worn by facilitators and support persons.
- Ensure that facilitators and support persons have access to a phone in case of emergency.
- Team members are not to be alone with children and young people (i.e. participants and junior assistants) where they cannot be seen by others. Keep areas open with team members visible. For example, do not shut blinds or curtains in this situation.
- Do not initiate physical contact with children or young people (i.e. participants and junior assistants). When responding to appropriate physical contact initiated by younger participants, a shoulder hug, a pat on the back or a hand-hold are the only appropriate responses.
- Facilitators are to plan activities and responses are to be anticipated. If the participants become increasingly difficult to manage during an activity the Lead Facilitator is to stop the activity and regain management of the situation e.g. stop the activity and have the participants return to their desks.
- The Lead Facilitator is to have a key contact person's details within the hosting organisation which is available in case of emergency or where an immediate concern is identified e.g. the classroom teacher. In a school in NSW Australia, if a reportable or potential reportable child protection matter arises, a person is required to tell the principal directly.
- Facilitators and support persons are to be fully aware of their hosting organisation and venue protocols including:
    - Evacuation and lock down procedures.
    - First aid procedures for the venue, and
    - Location of bathrooms.
- Debrief with the team after each session e.g. What worked well? What can be improved? Are there any concerns about a child or young person? Are there any concerns about the venue? It is important concerns are documented and referrals made where needed.

COMMUNICATION WITH CHILDREN AND YOUNG PEOPLE

- Junior assistants are to come under the definition of children and young people.
- Children and young people (i.e. participants and junior assistants) are to go to bathrooms and/or other enclosed areas in groups and are not to go alone. Adult team members are not to be in the bathroom at the same time as children and young people.
- Where a hosting organisation employee has not remained with the group e.g. the classroom teacher, participants need to be able to describe procedures for arriving and departing each session e.g. the Lead Facilitator will meet participants at their classroom; the classroom teacher will return at the end of the session, or the Lead Facilitators will take the participants to their designated playground area with the teacher on duty being advised that they have arrived.

COMMUNICATION WITH PARENT(S)/GUARDIAN(S) AND HOSTING ORGANISATION CONTACTS

- Intentionally communicate clearly and openly with the hosting organisation's key contacts e.g. principal, classroom teacher, school counsellor, about the program and the children and young persons' (i.e. participants and junior assistants) participation. Build relationships that are strong, positive and helpful.
- Discuss with the hosting organisation about the best way of intentionally communicating with parent(s)/guardian(s) about the program and their child's (i.e. participant or junior assistant) participation. Resources may be prepared by facilitator(s), however, **a key contact from the hosting organisation is to take on the responsibility of communicating directly with parent(s)/guardian(s).**
- Work with your hosting organisation contact e.g. classroom teacher, to determine a registration process for each child (i.e. participants and junior assistants). All children and young people should be signed in and out of each session.
- Have regular debriefs with your hosting organisation's key contact person.

ADDITIONAL REQUIREMENTS

A hosting organisation will generally require that all ShineGIRL team members complete an induction and confirm that they have read and understood the material provided to them during their induction.

For example, a school may have all facilitator(s) and support person(s) complete an 'Acknowledgment by school community member' form or equivalent (applicable to your country, state or territory).

ACKNOWLEDGMENT BY SCHOOL COMMUNITY MEMBER:

I *(insert full name)* _____

Being engaged by the School in the following role *(insert position)* _____

Hereby acknowledge that I:

- Have received the Child Protection Policy and the School Code of Conduct for staff, students and volunteers.

- Have read the Child Protection Policy and the School Code of Conduct for staff, students and volunteers and am obliged to comply with the Code and Policy, including any amendments made by the School from time to time.

- Am obliged to notify the School if my Working With Children Check status changes from 'Cleared'.

- Am a Mandatory Reporter of concerns about children or young people being at risk of significant harm.

- Am obliged to inform the Principal of suspicion of reportable conduct of another community member.

- Have received training in all aspects of the Child Protection Policy.

- Am aware that a current copy of the Child Protection Code of Conduct and Child Protection Policy is posted on the School's website.

_____   _____
Signature   Date

Outworking a Session

Brief

Allow time to brief your team on the plan for the session. Communication is vital for the team to operate well together. Make sure each team member knows what is required of them and that all tasks are delegated. Giving people responsibility means they are empowered to contribute. Participants can tell when a team is operating cohesively and when it is not.

Budget

Be creative with the budget you have. Recycle materials and, where possible, involve your community. Encourage people in your organisation, friends, family and community members to assist you in collecting recycled materials for use in session activities.

Prepare

Preparation for a ShineGIRL program takes time, organisation and thought. Every aspect of team member preparation can be used to create an atmosphere of value for participants. Where you intend to use music during a session, plan when the music will be played and at what volume. If you choose to use music with lyrics, listen carefully to the lyric before the session to ensure its suitability e.g. no explicit language or inappropriate content/references.

PRACTICAL TIPS FOR PREPARATION.

- Know your session content and program aims.
- Have the required resources for the session prepared in advance, and
- Have current knowledge of your Child Well-Being and Safety requirements for your group and venue (refer to Child Well-Being and Safety, pp. 15-25).

Being organised and mentally prepared will help each team member remain focused and present with their program group.

Set-up

One of the key ways to demonstrate value to the participants is doing everything with excellence. Each session will require time to prepare resources and set-up the room. Ensure you arrive at your venue at least 20-minutes before you are due to start.

The presentation of the room can create a responsive, warm, friendly and open atmosphere and this is often the first thing the participants will encounter. Setting-up the room differently to regular classes or activities can create anticipation. It also shows that you believe the participants are worth the effort of arriving early and preparing the room nicely. This adds another layer to communicate value. Changing the room can increase learning capacity, create anticipation and lift expectations if done well.

Basic items can make a huge difference to the way the room looks. You can be as creative as you like but do not make it complicated. Simply placing the session title on the board can stir-up curiosity.

Always consider the needs of individual participants in your program group. You may have a participant who experiences some difficulty in the sensory environment such as a participant:

- Who may not be able to differentiate foreground from background noise.
- Where an increase in visual stimuli or a change to the room environment may result in sensory overstimulation.

For example, if working in a school, seek advice from the classroom teacher and/or the school counsellor.

PRACTICAL TIPS FOR SET-UP

- Keep the set-up design simple and modern.
- Make sure the room is safe, uncluttered and comfortable.
- Consider lighting, sound and positioning of furniture.
- Ensure the room set-up is conducive to effective class management.

IMPLEMENTATION

Give full attention and energy to your program group (this includes only using a mobile phone for emergencies). Here are some things to remember:

- Exude a friendly attitude
- Foster an environment where all participants can contribute
- Give clear directions and keep the group on task
- Draw out ideas and input from the group
- Actively listen to participants and other team members
- Be sensitive and non-judgemental
- Encourage the group to discover together
- Scaffold participants' learning

Participant Assessment

The Lead Facilitator can use formative assessment, which is the process of gathering feedback during the sessions to assess if a participant is achieving the session outcomes. The teaching and learning activities are structured to enable the participants to achieve the outcomes. Formative assessment tools include the facilitator:

- Receiving informal feedback as a participant works through activities and contributes to group discussions, and
- Having each participant keep a portfolio of selected work from the sessions.

Where the program forms a part of an integrated unit of work in a school, the classroom teacher can put in place assessment tasks to further enable them to evaluate the effectiveness of the teaching and learning.

Clean-up

Clean-up is an important part of running your program with excellence. Clean-up includes:

- Cleaning resources e.g. paintbrushes.
- Neatly packing away resources for use in future sessions e.g. posters, and
- Tidying and returning the room to the way it was (or better!).

Debrief

Debriefing after each session allows the team to reflect and evaluate the session and prepare for the following week. Debriefing allows the team to identify what worked well and what can be improved upon and encourages personal reflection. If you have a specialist support person for your program, include them in this debrief. You may include assistants in the first part of the debrief but allow time for facilitator(s) and specialist support person(s) to have the opportunity to discuss any specific group concerns confidentially.

Follow-up

If you were asked a question during a session that you did not know the answer to:

- Make note of this (so you don't forget!)
- Research your response, and
- Plan your answer before the next session.

Where a concern is identified about a participant, follow your organisation's Child Well-Being and Safety policies that meet your country, state or territories requirements (refer to Child Well-Being and Safety, pp.15-25). Where a concern is identified about the venue, notify the person responsible.

SHINEGIRL

session outcomes.

Each session allows girls to participate in an experiential and interactive activity and have the opportunity to socially interact and connect with participants and facilitators.

worth.
SESSION 1: I AM VALUABLE
By the end of this session, each girl will be able to:
Gain an understanding of the concept of value
Identify what she personally values and why
Develop an awareness of personal value.

SESSION 2: I AM ONE-OF-A-KIND
By the end of this session, each girl will be able to:
Recognise the value of being one-of-a-kind
Distinguish the difference between uniqueness and comparison.

SESSION 3: I AM WONDERFULLY MADE
By the end of this session, each girl will be able to:
Have an understanding of the Worth concept
Identify ways to value herself.

strength.
SESSION 4: I HAVE THE POWER OF CHOICE
By the end of this session, each girl will be able to:
Explore and understand that she is born with feelings
Demonstrate skills required to enhance the power of choice

SESSION 5: MY DECISIONS DETERMINE MY DESTINATION
By the end of this session, each girl will be able to:
Apply and practise decision-making and problem-solving skills
Identify ways to display respect to themselves and others.

SESSION 6: I HAVE RESILIENCE
By the end of this session, each girl will be able to:
Recognise the value of developing resilience.

purpose.
SESSION 7: MY POTENTIAL IS LIMITLESS
By the end of this session, each girl will be able to:
Recognise the value of a positive environment for her potential to grow
Identify ways to build her confidence.

SESSION 8: MY LIFE HAS PURPOSE
By the end of this session, each girl will be able to:
Identify personal desires
Develop an understanding that she has something to contribute.

shine.
SESSION 9: SHINE!
By the end of this session, each girl will be able to:
Describe what she has learnt.

It is important to reinforce the foundational concepts throughout the sessions, to reveal the truth that the life of every individual girl counts and that she has intrinsic value.

SHINEGIRL

SP

session plans.

Session Plans.

ShineGIRL is designed to be presented in nine, 60-minute weekly sessions. This can be adapted to other formats if necessary. In a school environment it is usually conducted as one session per week during one or two high school periods. The format is designed to enable the sessions to be adapted to other timeframes with ease.

The sessions are flexible in delivery, order and style of presentation; however, we recommend maintaining the order where possible. The key is to creatively express the specific concept each week and to create an environment where girls experience and have understanding about the concepts presented.

Introduce the foundational concept at the beginning of each session, reinforcing it throughout and concluding each session with a brief overview of the concept by asking questions or giving the girls an opportunity to ask questions.

FOUNDATIONAL CONCEPT
Everything we say and all the activities we do should relate to the three foundational concepts:
Worth, Strength and Purpose.

Session Plans.

The following are the ingredients of the actual sessions:

ICEBREAKER
Each session begins with an icebreaker relevant to the concept. You can investigate the web for icebreakers and energisers or see the alternative icebreakers in Appendix A. Icebreakers capture the attention of the participants. Its purpose is to 'break the ice' through a fun activity at the start of the session so the girls are ready to receive, engage and get involved in the rest of the session.

POWER FOCUS
This is used to open up and introduce the concept and topic. It's designed to be specific and sharp and can include definitions, brainstorming or illustrations. For example, for the WORTH session 'I am valuable' we would introduce the title of the session along with a brief explanation of the session topic 'I am valuable'.

LAYING THE FOUNDATION
This is where the session outcomes are explained and the concept and topic is launched through illustrations, group discussion and demonstrations. Recommended teaching time is a maximum of 10 minutes.

PRESENTATION
This is the primary practical activity to achieve the outcomes. It is a chance for girls to 'experience' and 'practise' the concept presented. Professionals can also be organised to present on the topic. Recommended time is 30 minutes.

SMALL GROUP DISCUSSION
Get the girls to break up into small groups for the last 5 – 10 minutes of every session. Where possible, the girls should stay in the same small group with the same facilitator for the entire message. Small groups are a great opportunity to connect with the girls. This is the assessment component to establish if outcomes were achieved. Ask the girls questions that will help to summarise, recap and wrap up the session. Encourage the girls to share what they have learnt.

SHINE FACTOR
This is the special extra we give each girl to communicate the message of value. These gifts should relate to the session. Quotes or a key message from the session allow the girls to take something positive home with them. It creates a positive memory and enhances learning. It's up to you how creative you can be. Examples of ideas are included in each session plan.

'BODY AND SOUL, I AM WONDERFULLY MADE'

worth.

SESSION ONE I AM VALUABLE
SESSION TWO I AM ONE-OF-A-KIND
SESSION THREE I AM WONDERFULLY MADE

BASIS. 'BODY AND SOUL, I AM WONDERFULLY MADE.'

Introduction.

The basis for the module of 'I have WORTH' is for the girls to not only encounter their worth but to value themselves; to learn and to increase the ways they value their physical selves – the face, hands, hair, body and so forth in times of change (puberty being the time all changes begin). This transition in identity during adolescence could be challenging for both themselves and their parents. However, negotiating the changes from a place of value (knowledge and understanding) is empowerment.

To understand this concept, it means that it doesn't take status, reputation, honour, education, material richness, the latest fashions in our wardrobe and so forth to determine the worth inside of us. Even when everything else is stripped away from us, we have WORTH and will always have WORTH! We have it even now!

The WORTH concept explores:

i have worth!
i am valuable! i am one-of-a-kind!
i am wonderfully made!

i am VALUABLE

We are not rubbish and we are not a mistake.

Our value has nothing to do with what we think or what people say about us. Our value is not attached to our performance. It is not based on our circumstances, family background, religion or socio-economic status.

Our value is linked to our very being – it is intrinsic. Value cannot be earned, regardless of what circumstances we find ourselves in; we all qualify for value and worth.

When something is valuable, it is precious and one-of-a-kind; a treasure…it has worth.

Each of us is set apart as unique; there is no one else like us! We are born one-of-a-kind, custom-built and a masterpiece!

UNIQUE

| *yoo*-neek |

A one-off, original, exceptional, rare, unequalled, extraordinary, incomparable, matchless, individual.

We are all different! This is something to celebrate.

DIFFERENT

| dif-er-*uh* nt |

Not the same, unlike, of other nature, form or quality.

i am ONE-OF-A-KIND

Each of us was born with a one-of-a-kind personality. The way we love is one-of-a-kind. Our personal style and creativity is one-of-a-kind. How we communicate is different. How we write or give expression to something is unique. If a group of people were to write about the same topic, not one paper would be written the same. That is because our personal expression of life is unique and one-of-a-kind.

i am WONDERFULLY *made.*

There are many facets and details of who we are. Every part of us has a purpose and a function. Our mind, body, emotions, personality, character, passions and dreams are all intricate parts of us.

There are many characteristics that contribute to our individuality; our strengths, talents, laughter and smile have all been uniquely designed just for us. No one else is exactly the same. We have been designed just the way we are for a reason and a purpose.

When we love something, we value it. Anything we love and adore, we treat with value.
When we love ourselves, we are valuing ourselves.

facilitator information.

The WORTH activities engage the girls in a personal and intimate way and encourage them to embrace their natural one-of-a-kind beauty. The activities are non-confrontational, tactile ways to engage and connect participants with each other and the facilitators; building relationship and rapport, and creating trust and openness, which is required for the Strength and Purpose sessions to be effective.

These activities are not the focus for the sessions, but rather messages used to complement and accelerate the participants' learning of the Worth concept. They enable you to create a move into an organic practical experience in the classroom based on the school, girls, teachers, culture and environment. We are after the EXPERIENCE and the SKILL.

All activities are designed to reinforce the foundational concept that each participant has value. Any activities undertaken within the WORTH sessions should reinforce this concept. Reiterate to the girls that the stage of puberty is a natural, organic process of change, and it's a privilege and an exciting time!

"We have worth and will always have worth!"

'BODY AND SOUL, I AM WONDERFULLY MADE'

1

worth.

SESSION ONE I AM VALUABLE

MATERIAL REQUIRED: Money note, 'I am valuable' handouts (see Appendix B to C), name badges, jewels x 2, brown paper bag, beautiful box for jewel, whiteboard markers, whiteboard. HAND MASSAGE MATERIALS: Paper towels, raw sugar and oil (baby oil or olive oil), exfoliation product or hand cream, bowls (for sugar and oil)

Please see recommended layout below.

ACTIVITY	DETAILS	NOTES/MATERIALS
Introduction (15 mins)	Introduce the team. Explain the message and the outcomes. Ask the girls to introduce themselves and explain what they are expecting from Shine. Establish group guidelines.	Come up with some group guidelines that can be displayed on the whiteboard.
Icebreaker Options (10 mins)	ACTIVITIES: Two truths and a lie Box of truth The questionnaire game Ask the facilitator	
Power Focus (5 mins)	'I AM VALUABLE'	
Laying The Foundation (5 mins)	Give expression to being valuable Group Discussion: You are valuable Demonstration: Local currency note Illustration: Jewel in paper bag vs. jewel in beautiful box	RESOURCES: money note, 2 x jewels, paper bag, beautiful box, big piece of paper, coloured permanent markers.
Presentation (20 mins)	Group Discussion: How do hands relate to value? Group Discussion: Caring for our hands Group Activity: Hand massage	RESOURCES: oil, raw sugar, bowls or hand cream, handouts, whiteboard markers, whiteboard.
Small Group Discussion (5 mins)	Q. What can you do to show someone in your life that they are valuable? Q. What have you learnt about your own value today? Reinforce WORTH concept 'I AM VALUABLE'.	
Shine Factor	As you give out the gifts, encourage each girl.	Gifts

outcomes.
By the end of this session, each girl will be able to:

GAIN AN UNDERSTANDING OF THE CONCEPT OF VALUE

IDENTIFY WHAT SHE PERSONALLY VALUES AND WHY

DEVELOP AN AWARENESS OF PERSONAL VALUE

introduction.

All ShineGIRL team members are to introduce themselves and share why they are on team.

Introduce the 3 foundational concepts to the girls, WORTH, STRENGTH & PURPOSE, and briefly explain each concept. Encourage the girls to introduce themselves especially if they don't already know each other. Build expectation.

shineGIRL group guidelines.

Establish Group Guidelines with the girls. You can do this by:

- Using your organisation or hosting organisations existing Group Guidelines (sometimes these will already be on a poster on the wall!)
- Collaborating with the girls to develop guidelines specific to that program group. You should write these on a poster at the front of the room and bring them along to future sessions. Here is an example of Group Guidelines:
  - Arrive on time
  - Listen while others are speaking
  - Follow safety instructions
  - Mobile phones on silent and away
  - Stay calm
  - Be involved

When an individual girl needs a directive to correct poor behaviour, be clear and firm, without expressing anger. Where possible, speak to the participant quietly. If a situation is escalating or becomes unsafe, always ask for help from a supervisor or other adult team member. In a school context, seek immediate support from school staff.

icebreakers.

ACTIVITY: TWO TRUTHS AND A LIE

Going around the circle, each girl and facilitator is to say their name and three statements about themselves, two of them have to be true and one has to be false. The rest of the class guesses which statement is false.

ACTIVITY: BOX OF TRUTH
Going around the circle, each girl has to pick a question from the box and read it out. They then get to choose if they want to answer it themselves or give it to someone else in the circle to answer. Each girl is to answer one question. Examples of questions are:
- What is your favourite food?
- What makes you smile?
- What is your biggest fear?
- If you could go out to dinner with anyone in the world, who would you choose?
- What are 3 words that describe you?
- Where do you wish you were right now?
- What is the most common compliment that you get?

ACTIVITY: THE QUESTIONNAIRE GAME
- Hand the questionnaire to each of the girls and facilitators (see Appendix B).
- Ask them to fill in the left box about their favourite things. (Give them a timeframe to complete it.)
- The girls and facilitators then need to find someone else in the class who has the same answer as them. (Encourage a good atmosphere and set an example by walking around to each person).

Once everyone has had enough time to go around to each person, ask the girls to take their seats. Ask the girls if anyone was able to find someone for each of their answers. You may want to give out prizes. PURPOSE: We are all unique. You may have had a lot of similar answers to other girls, but you still would have had some differences.

ACTIVITY: ASK THE FACILITATOR
So now that you have had the chance to find out a bit about each of the girls, it is their chance to find out more about you. Hand out a Post it note to each girl. (Use bright colours if possible). Ask the girls to each write down one question they would like to ask you. It can be a personal question or they may want your advice on something they are going through. Collect the questions in a beautiful box or bowl. The facilitators should take turns pulling a question out and answering it.

power focus.
I AM VALUABLE

There are no mistakes! Life is created with a purpose and a reason for existence. No one has been created by mistake. Our value has nothing to do with what we think or what people say about us. Our value is not attached to our performance. It is not based on our circumstances, family background, religion or socio-economic status. Human value is not determined by what people say about us. It's not determined by whether or not we have failed more times than we have succeeded. Our value is not determined by whether or not we have finished school, have a job, a car, are in a relationship or are popular. Circumstances such as if we are sick or healthy, rich or poor do not determine our value.

Our value is linked to our very being – it is intrinsic. Value cannot be earned, regardless of what circumstances we find ourselves in, we all qualify for value and worth.

Explore the questions: 'Am I accepted? Do I matter? Do you see me? Do you hear me? Does what I am saying matter to you? Do you recognise me? Do your eyes light up when I am around?' Every one of us has this need for acceptance. It's a universal need. You matter! What you have to say matters. You are worth being cared about, listened to and validated. You are recognised. You are important.

we are all PRICELESS

laying the foundation.

GROUP DISCUSSION: YOU ARE VALUABLE

Emphasise to the girls that living a life of value embraces the (young) woman that is emerging and gives her space to grow. Puberty is an adventure and it only lasts for a short while.

DEMONSTRATION: LOCAL CURRENCY NOTE – FOR EXAMPLE, $5 OR $10.

Here is a $10 note. What if I scrunched up this $10? What about if I stepped on it, crinkled it up and got it dirty? Would its value change? No, its value remains the same even if it isn't treated with care. No matter what happens to you, whether you have been treated well or you have been mistreated, you have not lost your value. We are valuable and we remain valuable.

ILLUSTRATION: JEWEL IN PAPER BAG VS. JEWEL IN BEAUTIFUL BOX

Hand out two jewels to two participants. One scrunched up in a paper bag, the other wrapped in a beautiful box. Ask them to both open up what they were given. Inside both is a jewel that carries exactly the same value. So no matter what's on the outside, intrinsically, we have this treasure inside that carries weight.

presentation- value outworked

GROUP DISCUSSION: HOW DO HANDS RELATE TO VALUE?

Hands were never designed to cause harm to ourselves or to others. Hands are an extension of our gifts and talents into the world. Our hands are designed to serve us well and serve others well in love.

A hurting humanity can end up having hands that hurt others, but it's not what our hands are meant to be doing. Hands are only one part of our amazing body. They are never insignificant and add to our worth as a human being. Every hand not only looks unique and is one-of-a-kind but every hand does unique things.

GROUP DISCUSSION: CARING FOR OUR HANDS

Explain interesting facts about hands (see Appendix C for handout sheet)
Brainstorm either in small groups or all together:
- What do we use our hands for?
- What are some things hands can do for people – helping and giving?

The demonstration below is only one example of our unique one-of-a-kind nature and individual form.

GROUP ACTIVITY: HAND MASSAGE

Use an exfoliating hand scrub or hand cream for this activity.

EXFOLIATING HAND SCRUB:
- Make sure everyone has easy access to hand towels and locate where the nearest sink is.
- Ask the team to explain the activity, including what is in the scrub and the benefits of exfoliating regularly.
- As an alternative to a product scrub, you can use baby oil or olive oil and raw sugar.
- Mix some oil with raw sugar and keep it a thick consistency.
- Give each girl a tablespoon full of the scrub.
- Ask the girls in their pairs to massage the scrub into the other's hands.

HAND MASSAGE:
Pass around hand cream for each girl to give themselves a hand massage. Be aware of sensitive skin.

small group discussion.
This is each facilitator's first opportunity to meet with their small group. Use this time to encourage the girls for a few minutes and tell them how excited you are to be doing the ShineGIRL program with them.

Q. What can you do to show someone in your life that they are valuable?
Q. What have you learnt about your own value today?

ASSESS OUTCOMES
Reinforce the WORTH concept. Affirm the group as a whole or to each individual by name – 'I am valuable.' This exercise is a powerful way to end the session.

shine factor.
IDEAS: Give gifts that relate to hands, such as hand or nail cream, exfoliating hand scrub or a henna tattoo.

note to facilitator.
Be creative with the room set-up to create anticipation and atmosphere. This activity is a great opportunity for the facilitators to connect with the participants. Look out for girls who may need extra care and encouragement.

'BODY AND SOUL, I AM WONDERFULLY MADE'

2
worth.

SESSION TWO I AM ONE-OF-A-KIND

MATERIAL REQUIRED:
Shine Factor, name badges, whiteboard markers, whiteboard, picture of Mona Lisa, big piece of blank paper.
FACE/HAIR MATERIALS: Disposable wipes, small dishes, tissues and cotton wool balls, cleanser, moisturiser, sunscreen, hair bands, elastics, clips, bobby pins, mirrors, hair gel, mousse, oils, spray, combs, brushes.

Please see recommended layout below.

ACTIVITY	DETAILS	NOTES/MATERIALS
Icebreaker Options (10 mins)	Activity: Signature	Whiteboard or hand out some paper.
Power Focus (5 mins)	'I AM ONE-OF-A-KIND'	
Laying The Foundation (10 mins)	Illustration: Mona Lisa Group Discussion: One-of-a-kind is beautiful	
Presentation (30 mins)	Activity: Staying fresh and highlighting your natural shine (face/hair)	Hand out any relevant information and supplies to take the time to look after our face/hair.
Discussion and Wrap-Up (5 mins)	Q. What is a one-of-a-kind feature that you like about yourself? Q. Why do you think living a one-of-a-kind life is important? Reinforce WORTH concept 'I AM ONE-OF-A-KIND'.	
Shine Factor	Give away the gift they made to another girl in the group.	Gifts

outcomes.
By the end of this session, each girl will be able to:

RECOGNISE THE VALUE OF BEING ONE-OF-A-KIND

DISTINGUISH THE DIFFERENCE BETWEEN UNIQUENESS AND COMPARISON.

one-of-a-kind is
BEAUTIFUL

icebreaker.
ACTIVITY: GIVE EXPRESSION TO OUR ONE-OF-A-KIND SIGNATURE

Put a piece of butcher's paper in the middle of the table. Ask the girls to write their signature down. Emphasise the difference in handwriting and signatures. Once everyone has completed their signature, ask the girls to stand back and look at all the drawings. No signature is the same.

Discuss with the girls how they can give expression to their one-of-a-kind life. Ask the girls to draw lines from their signature with the below questions for them to think about.

- How does my appearance give expression to my one-of-a-kind life?
- How does my heritage and culture give expression to my one-of-a-kind life?
- How does my personality and character give expression to my one-of-a-kind life?
- How does my personal written signature give expression to my one-of-a-kind life?

The participants may not be able to answer these questions easily, and that is okay. Use the questions as a discussion point to further unpack this concept of being one-of-a-kind. Everyone has a different way of expressing their signature. Their signature is an expression of who they are; their personal style and their creativity. We are all responsible for bringing out the signature message in us. (For alternative icebreakers see Appendix A.)

SIGNATURE | sig-n*uh*-cher |

One-of-a-kind style, personality, culture, heart, passion and vocation.

power focus.
'I AM ONE-OF-A-KIND.'

When something is one-of-a-kind, it is precious and valuable; it is a treasure... it has worth. Each of us is set apart as unique and there is no one like us! We are born one-of-a-kind, custom-built and a masterpiece!

UNIQUE

| *yoo*-neek |

A one-off, original, exceptional, rare, unequalled, extraordinary, incomparable, matchless, individual.

We are all different! This is something to celebrate.

DIFFERENT

| dif-er-*uh* nt |

Not the same, unlike, of other nature, form or quality.

Conforming to what society and popular culture says is beautiful only steals from our uniqueness and creates sameness about every human being that is false and a thief to our identity. Also, sameness robs the world of the treasured one-of-a-kind way we were formed. We are made unique for a reason, and that is to fit the one-of-a-kind purpose, also uniquely designed for us. The truth is we are all beautiful. Human life is beautiful and the form of a human being is the most significant and wonderful thing.

When we embrace and love who we are, value the way we are made and care for ourselves, it shows our significance. We know we count for much. We know we are beautiful just the way we are, just the way we are meant to be; perfect for such a time as this.

Also, each of us has a one-of-a-kind personality. The way we love is one-of-a-kind. Our personal style and creativity is one-of-a-kind. How we communicate is different. How we write or give expression to something is unique. If a group of people were to write about the same topic, not one paper would be written the same. That is because our personal expression of life is unique and one-of-a-kind.

You matter! What you have to say matters. You are worth being cared about, listened to and validated. You are recognised. You are important.

laying the foundation.

ILLUSTRATION: MONA LISA

Use a paper copy of the Mona Lisa as an example of how much more the original is worth than a copy. The Mona Lisa is valuable because it is an original. Its value is reflected by the way it is treated. Any copy from the original is not worth the same as what the original is worth.

You are an original. Your worth comes from you being a one-off.
You cannot be compared, cloned or replaced.

GROUP DISCUSSION: ONE-OF-A-KIND IS BEAUTIFUL!

Comparison is a real issue that many, if not all girls struggle with at one time or another.
EMBRACE – accept and love who you are.
CELEBRATE – enjoy the differences people have to offer.

We begin to compare ourselves to others when we feel inadequate or insecure about who we truly are. Our individuality carries great worth, and because of this we don't need to compare, change or modify who we are to fit the mould of someone else.

As a group, discuss the following questions:
- What things do we compare ourselves to? What is unhealthy comparison?
- What is the difference between comparison and being inspired by someone?
- Who is someone you look up to? Are inspired by? Why?

Write the participants' responses on the board. The facilitator can share their personal examples if it will help with the group discussion.

presentation.
'value yourself because you are one-of-a-kind.'

ACTIVITY: STAYING FRESH AND HIGHLIGHTING YOUR SHINE

Discuss what 'staying fresh' means and how good it feels when skin and hair is clean. You may also want to talk about:
- Washing your hands before handling food items
- How to manage menstrual cycles
- Coaching on skin care (cleansing, moisturising, sunscreen, as well as skin types and how to handle acne), hygiene (deodorant, oral care) and hair care (shampoo, conditioning, styling)
- How marketing and magazines may form thoughts about beauty that lead to wearing make-up because you may not feel good about yourself
- Being breast-aware.[12]

Emphasise to the girls that all these activities are simply basic health and beauty tips that can either be learnt from friends and magazines or in a classroom environment.

At the beginning of this activity, emphasise the uniqueness of each individual and the fact that we are all one-of-a-kind and that is what gives us worth. Then, divide the class into groups of four and distribute the resources. This can be done around one big cluster of tables.

For the face, this is a great opportunity to invite a skin care specialist to demonstrate the techniques on a willing student volunteer. Emphasise that the skin is the largest organ in the body and worth caring for.

Topics to cover include:
- A simple outline on what 'skin' is
- Different skin types and how to care for them
- The importance of water for healthy skin
- The importance of good nutrition for healthy skin
- A daily process of cleansing, moisturising and sunscreen
- Face masks – organic (homemade) or commercial
- Skin protection from sun damage
- The normality of skin changes and how to handle acne
- Hygiene tips

12 For more information, please view
http://www.mcgrathfoundation.com.au/images/files/BreastAwareBrochureA4.pdf

ACTIVITY: GIVE EXPRESSION TO OUR ONE-OF-A-KIND FEATURES.

Hand out photocopies of black and white faces (2 faces per girl). Encourage the girls to colour in the faces with eye shadow and blush or permanent markers. For one face, ask the girls to be as creative as they want. For the other face, ask the girls to make a face with a more 'natural' look. Once everyone has completed their pieces of art, encourage the girls to look at each other's masterpieces. Also, discuss the fact that if they do wear make-up, it should only be used to enhance their beauty, as they are already beautiful from within. Make-up should not be used to cover or change who we are or to be worn as a mask. Make-up as a function is to simply bring out and express our uniqueness. However, make-up can also create problems with image, if it's used to cover yourself up or if it gets to the point where you can't seem to live without it at all.

For hair care, this is a great opportunity to invite a hairdresser to demonstrate how to look after your hair on a willing student volunteer. However, cutting is not permitted.

The topics to cover include:
- A great cut and style
- Shampooing and conditioning
- Perms and colour
- Helpful hints on the cause of hair stress.

See Appendix D for a hair care handout.

discussion and wrap-up.

Q. What is a one-of-a-kind feature that you like about yourself?
Q. Why do you think living a one-of-a-kind life is important?

Girls can often find it hard talking about what they like about themselves. Encourage them to push through. If someone is struggling to answer the question, ask the group if anyone wants to suggest a feature they admire about the person. Reinforce the WORTH concept. Affirm the group as a whole or to each individual by name – 'I am one-of-a-kind.'

ASSESS OUTCOMES

shine factor.

IDEAS: Small hygiene packs

note to facilitator.

We would like to focus on homemade natural products as much as possible to make it fun, interesting and low cost. Avoid talking about 'good' and 'bad' skin. It really is all about feeling comfortable with the skin that belongs uniquely to each of us, i.e. colour, type, beauty spots, freckles, texture and complexion.

'BODY AND SOUL, I AM WONDERFULLY MADE'

3

worth.

SESSION THREE | I AM WONDERFULLY MADE

MATERIAL REQUIRED: A Teacup Story handout, Paper, whiteboard markers, whiteboard, cardboard, pens, Shine factor. HEALTH MATERIALS; Examples of healthy food, recipes. ENERGY ITEMS: Water bottle, sports trainers, t-shirts, sports hats, sports equipment.

Please see recommended layout below.

ACTIVITY	DETAILS	NOTES/MATERIALS
Icebreaker (5 mins)	Activity: WORTH acronym	RESOURCES: whiteboard, markers.
Power Focus (10 mins)	'I AM WONDERFULLY MADE' Illustration: A Teacup Story	RESOURCES: a teacup story handout (see Appendix E).
Laying The Foundation (10 mins)	Group Discussion: The Body – wonderfully made! Describe the different facets of the body, discuss questions as a group.	
Presentation (25 mins)	Emphasise that health, nutrition and fitness will do more for a young girl's well-being. So don't have them just as options, but core to what this session is about. Activities: Health Energy	RESOURCES: equipment for activity.
Small Group Discussion (10 mins)	Discuss WORTH acronym handout in small groups. Reinforce WORTH concept 'I AM WONDERFULLY MADE'.	
Shine Factor	As you give out the gifts, encourage each girl	Gifts

outcomes.
By the end of this session, each girl will be able to:
EXPLAIN HER UNDERSTANDING OF THE WORTH CONCEPT
IDENTIFY WAYS TO VALUE HERSELF.

icebreaker.
ACTIVITY: WORTH ACRONYM

Have the participants pair up and come up with an acronym for WORTH. Share their responses in the group. For example:

W   Wonderful, Well-being
O   Original, One-of-a-kind
R   Real, Radiant
T   Treasured, Transforming
H   Healthy, Hope

power focus.
'I AM WONDERFULLY MADE'

There are many facets to who we are. Every part of us has a purpose and a function. Our mind, body, emotions, personality, character, passions and dreams are all intricate parts of who we are.

There are many characteristics that contribute to our individuality: our strengths, talents, laughter and smile have all been uniquely designed just for us. No one else is exactly the same.

We have been designed just the way we are for a reason and a purpose.

The idea of living a life that shines is to see all that we do be about placing value on ourselves and others. We exercise to be strong in the core of our body, so that we can be fit to carry on our amazing journey well. We require fuel for the body by eating the right food to keep healthy, as well as limiting chemicals where possible that are harmful for our inner and outer environment. So when we love something, we value it. Anything we love and adore, we treat with value. When we love ourselves, we are valuing ourselves.

*Ask two to three girls
to volunteer to read a teacup story*
(See Appendix E)

A TEA CUP *story*

A couple went into an antique shop one day and found a beautiful teacup sitting on a shelf. They took it off the shelf, so they could look at it more closely, and said, "We really want to buy this gorgeous cup."

All of the sudden, the teacup began to talk, saying, "I wasn't always like this. There was a time when I was just a cold, hard, colourless lump of clay. One day my master picked me up and said, 'I could do something with this.' Then he started to pat me, and roll me, and change my shape."

"I said, 'What are you doing? That hurts. I don't know if I want to look like this! Stop!' But he said, 'Not yet.'

"Then he put me on a wheel and began to spin me around and around and around, until I screamed, 'Let me off, I am getting dizzy!' 'Not yet,' he said.

"Then he shaped me into a cup and put me in a hot oven. I cried, 'Let me out! It's hot in here, I am suffocating.' But he just looked at me through that little glass window and smiled and said, 'Not yet.'

"When he took me out, I thought his work on me was over, but then he started to paint me. I couldn't believe what he did next. He put me back into the oven, and I said, 'You have to believe me, I can't stand this! Please let me out!' But he said, 'Not yet.'

"Finally, he took me out of the oven and set me up on a shelf where I thought he had forgotten me. Then one day he took me off the shelf and held me before a mirror. I couldn't believe my eyes, I had become a beautiful teacup that everyone wants to buy."

AUTHOR UNKNOWN

laying the foundation.

GROUP DISCUSSION: THE BODY – WONDERFULLY MADE!

Random facts about the body:
- The human heart creates enough pressure when it pumps blood out to the body, that it could squirt blood 30 feet!
- No two outer ears (pinnae) – even your own – are exactly alike. There are some key identification points on the outer ear that do not change throughout one's life.
- Earology is the study of the external ear which, like fingerprints, shows a unique design from person to person.
- Man's one kilogram brain is the most complex and orderly arrangement of matter known in the universe.
- The human eye can distinguish about 17,000 different colours.
- When you sneeze, all your bodily functions stop, even your heart. It is impossible to sneeze and keep your eyes open at the same time.

Ask the group to describe all the different facets of the body. Write up their answers up on the board.

MIND – mental capacity
ORGANS – heart, liver, lungs, stomach, intestines, kidneys, bladder
OUTER BODY – skin, hair, nails
BLOOD – oxygen
PHYSICAL MOBILITY – arms, legs, neck, back, feet, hands, muscles
EMOTIONS – feelings
SUBCONSCIOUS AND CONSCIOUS THOUGHTS
KNOWLEDGE – the brain stores up information throughout our lifetime
AWARENESS – of our surroundings (we need it to drive a car)
ATMOSPHERE – we hold the power to create the right atmosphere
PERSONALITY – character traits
ATTITUDE – healthy or unhealthy attitudes towards self or others
EXPRESSION – sing, dance, body language, writing, talking, presentation

Our body is the main vessel that allows us to function. When we are sick, it restricts our ability to do everyday things. We realise how much we need our body when we are limited in what we can do. When we are healthy, we feel like we can do anything. Our body enables us to do the things we love doing; having fun, enjoying the company of others, studying, travelling, exercising etc. Our body helps us to outwork our dreams and desires.

Q. Do we truly value and appreciate our bodies?

Q. If our bodies are valuable to us, how should we look after them?

EYES – No one has been born with the same kind of eye. In the movies, we see the use of a person's iris to help identify each individual. No one sees life the way we do. We hold a unique perspective, a unique vision.

FEET – No one lives the same story. No one has walked the journey that we have. There is value to our story. Our journey can bring hope to others.

HANDS – Think about what we use our hands for. There are so many different purposes. Our hands have touched the lives of others. How we display our care for others is unique from anyone else. Our hands and the story they bring have value.

HEART – The heart is tender, fragile and precious. The words we speak come from our heart. How we love others and how we treat others will impact their lives in a powerful way.

HEAD – Inside our head is a brain that contains intelligence, creativity, insight and our thoughts. The way we think and see life is different from anyone else. We carry unique perspectives and creative thoughts.

SOUL – Our soul is the very core of our being. It is our emotions and our thoughts. Our personality and each characteristic create our unique core. Our soul is custom made for our body.

MOUTH – The way we communicate with others is unique. We all have a unique way of talking and communicating that reflects our character and personality.

Each of us are masterpieces, one-of-a-kind, custom-built for a wonderful purpose. Every detail of who we are was carefully thought and designed uniquely. None of us are a mistake; we all have a purpose, a destination that only we can fulfil.

presentation.

OPTIONS: There are 2 options for this session, Health or Energy. Choose the activity that best suits your target audience and make it come alive by ensuring the presentation is relevant to your group.

ACTIVITY: HEALTH

You are about to embark on an adventure that will lead you to greater personal understanding, more energy and a greater zest for life.

1. Go through nutritional information with the girls. Discuss: Benefits of eating a balanced meal with lots of fruit and fibre and less processed foods Vitamins we get from certain foods Effects of unhealthy eating.

Ask the girls to write down what they would eat on a weekly basis and discuss whether there are alternatives to unhealthy food.

2. For the health session, set the room up with colourful fruit platters for everyone, bottles of water and so forth. It is preferable to have a professional as your guest presenter for this activity, such as a nutritionist, doctor, nurse or health professional skilled in this area. We should not instruct on what we have no qualification for. You could also bring in a range of other different healthy foods for the girls to try (such as dried fruit and nuts, cereal, vegetables), or make a smoothie or fresh juice with the girls.

   *Check for allergies.

Always focus on health not image. We feel good when we are healthy. By eating healthy, we value our body.

ACTIVITY: ENERGY

1. Ask the girls about what form of exercise they do. It's best to exercise daily, whether it's walking the dog for 30 minutes or playing a team sport. Our muscles need to be exercised to keep definition and remain strong. When we exercise, we activate our happy endorphins which help keep our emotions in balance.

2. Encourage the girls to get involved in exercise activities such as Pilates, sit-ups, push-ups, stretches, lunges or exercises they can do with a partner.

For the Energy session, set the room up with a fitness theme or like a gym class with yoga mats. Display fitness items such as water bottles, sports trainers, t-shirts, sports hats, sports equipment (tennis racquet, tennis ball, basketball) and so forth.

Invite a qualified fitness instructor to attend. Plan the session with them beforehand. Ensure that the focus is on 'looking after ourselves because we are valuable'. Practise some exercises and draw up individual fitness plans for the girls.

Over exercising is as harmful to our bodies as no exercise. Balance is the key. It is essential for our bodies to have regular rest days to revitalise and restore the muscles we use. It is also important to emphasise that health is the most important focus here. The benefits of healthy eating and exercising come when they are a regular part of our lifestyle.

Basic principles of health at every size are:
- Accept and respect diversity of body shapes and sizes
- Recognise health and well-being as multi-dimensional, which includes physical, social, spiritual, occupational, emotional and intellectual.
- Promote all aspects of health and well-being for all sizes.
- Promote eating in a manner which balances individual nutritional needs, hunger and so forth.
- Promote life-enhancing physical activity in tune with your body type.[14]

small group discussion: WORTH acronym.

Give each girl a WORTH acronym handout. Discuss what is on the handout and have the girls add to their handbook the ideas the group had during the icebreaker activity. Girls can take their handouts home with them.

shine factor.

IDEAS: Healthy food, bottled water, 'I am wonderfully made' quote, and a nutrition fact sheet scrolled up with a ribbon.

note to facilitator.

If you or any of the group members have any particular personal or health concerns (physical, emotional health) about a participant, we recommend you speak to a teacher or counsellor.

---

14 Source: BodyMatters Australasia, www.bodymatters.com.au

'CHOOSE LIFE'

strength.

SESSION FOUR I HAVE THE POWER OF CHOICE
SESSION FIVE MY DECISIONS DETERMINE MY DESTINATION
SESSION SIX I HAVE RESILIENCE

BASIS. 'CHOOSE LIFE'

introduction.

Strength is the power within us that helps us rise above circumstances and adversity. Strength enables us to overcome our challenges. Life is not always smooth sailing. There will be some storms and high waves as well as calm waters in life. How we face the storms of life will determine the effect that it has on us.

Being able to overcome adversity and challenges is not just for us but for everyone. Our story of challenge and triumph can give hope and strength to others in situations similar to ours. Strength is for service.

Strength is like a muscle. If we don't use it, it will remain dormant, idle, unused. By using the strength within us, we are building and growing it as well as our character and personality.

Many of us carry around 'emotional' things that can weigh us down like heavy coats and bags. These weights are the baggage from our lives; the hurt, the pain, and the regrets. We have the choice to receive healing from our issues and to let go of our baggage.

Strength is exercising our power to choose. By exercising choices that help us live 'balanced', we build and develop our inner strength.

The Strength concept explores:

thoughts. feelings. choices.

i have the power of CHOICE.

We have a free will – the power to make choices in our lives. Strength comes when we make choices that benefit ourselves and others. Just like push-ups help build our physical strength, every time we make a good decision it is like doing a push-up for our soul. Inner strength comes from the daily decision to choose to do the right thing. The right choice for me in a certain situation may not be the right choice for you. We need to discover what is right for ourselves. And sometimes it can seem like there is no 'right choice'. It takes real strength in those situations to weigh up the consequences and make the best choice we can.

Choices affect our lives and the lives of people around us. No matter how we feel, we have the power to choose our direction in life. This does not mean choices will always be easy. Some of our choices will be challenging. Making right choices in life, especially in difficult situations, builds our strength and maturity as young girls. Our decisions can be influenced by others, especially those we love (family, friends, partners). For example, some teenage girls make decisions they regret because they feel pressured by their friends to do things they wouldn't normally do just so they can fit in. In situations like these, we can choose to either hand our 'power of choice' over to others or hold onto it ourselves.

No matter what happens in life, whether we feel powerless or not, we will always have the power of choice.
We have the CHOICE to: RESPOND to a situation or REACT to it.

my decisions determine my DESTINATION.

In every situation, in every day, we make choices. In those choices there are consequences that add to our life, moving us forward and there are consequences that stop us moving at all or cause us to move backwards. There are decisions that can fast track us on our journey and others that can keep us from our desired destination. Decisions we make give us control over our life, but they don't just affect our life, they also impact the people around us. There are choices that are selfish and those that are selfless.

All the decisions we make – from getting out of bed each morning to who we marry – have consequences. Our choices determine what our tomorrow will look like. Things we decide to overcome and things we decide to accept all have a direct effect on our life. Often we don't realise that it's the small, everyday decisions that get us to our desired destination.

i have
RESIL IENCE.

A strong person is able to stand firm whilst facing significant difficulties, as they have a strong sense of self-belief and faith to keep calm and carry on.

KEY MESSAGE TO REINFORCE THROUGH STRENGTH SESSIONS:

*i have strength! i have the power of choice!
my decisions determine my destination! i have resilience!*

'CHOOSE LIFE'

strength.

SESSION FOUR | I HAVE THE POWER OF CHOICE

MATERIAL REQUIRED: Feeling cards (see Appendix M), Fizzy drink bottle, whiteboard and markers, mirrors, 'I have the power of choice' handouts (see Appendix F), printed examples of ways to build strength, role play cards, pens and permanent markers, name badges

Please see recommended layout below.

ACTIVITY	DETAILS	NOTES/MATERIALS
Icebreaker (5 mins)	Activity: Discovering love languages	Resources: love heart cards
Power Focus (5 mins)	Group Discussion: What makes a person strong? 'I HAVE THE POWER OF CHOICE.' Activity: Ways to build strength into our lives	
Laying The Foundation (15 mins)	Emotions defined and explained	Resources: mirror
Presentation (30 mins)	Group Activities: Identifying feelings, Role play Activity: Managing your emotions Demonstration: Fizzy drink bottle Activity: Role play	Resources: equipment for activity
Small Group Discussion (5 mins)	Q. What did you learn from today's session? Q. How could you use or apply what you have learnt in your daily life? Reinforce STRENGTH concept 'I HAVE THE POWER OF CHOICE.'	
Shine Factor	As you give out the gifts, encourage each girl	Gifts

outcomes.
By the end of this session, each girl will be able to:
EXPLORE AND UNDERSTAND THAT SHE IS BORN WITH FEELINGS
DEMONSTRATE SKILLS REQUIRED TO ENHANCE THE POWER OF CHOICE.

icebreaker.
ACTIVITY: DISCOVERING LOVE LANGUAGES

Hand out one heart card to every participant (simply cut out some paper heart cards). Then ask everyone to write one thing that makes them feel happy or feel loved without showing the next person. Then on the other side of the heart, have the participant write their name and hand it over to you.

NOTE: This is a test of how much we all know each other.

Once the answer has been mentioned, the participants have to try and guess who it is... it could be anyone in the room.

power focus.
GROUP DISCUSSION:
WHAT MAKES A PERSON STRONG?

When you picture someone strong, you may think of someone with lots of muscles. Muscles make us strong on the outside, but in this session we focus on what makes us strong on the inside.

ACTIVITY: WAYS TO BUILD STRENGTH INTO OUR LIVES

Print these examples out for each girl to read. Discuss them as a group. Ask the girls if there are any particular statements they relate to and if they have any personal stories they would like to share with the group.

Such as, "Who has made a good decision? What was it and why was it 'good'?"

strength is...

- Making good decisions.
- Recognising our feelings/emotions.
- Respecting ourselves and others.
- Building healthy relationships.
- Being okay with making mistakes as long as we learn from them.
- Looking for the good in all things.
- Asking for help when we need it.
- Being thankful.
- Knowing what we stand for.
- Choosing to accept and love ourselves for who we are.

laying the foundation.

EMOTION | ih-moh-sh*uh* n |

Any strong feeling, such as joy or fear, the part of a person's character based on feelings rather than thought.
It's important to recognise how we are feeling.

1. DEFINE WHAT EMOTIONS ARE: Ask the girls to close their eyes and picture that they are travelling on a journey toward their desired destination. There are mountains and hills rising up, challenging the path they have chosen. Ask the girls to open their eyes and open discussion explaining that, often these mountains or hills can be our feelings and we can be unsure of how to navigate our way through them.

2. EXPLAIN THAT EMOTIONS ARE HEALTHY: Imagine going through life without feeling anything. Discuss what that would look like for each girl. Feelings give life richness and depth. All our emotions are a healthy indicator as to how we are feeling. We can feel different emotions each hour of the day! Each feeling we have tells us what is happening on the inside. We may feel angry, sad, joyful, hopeful or peaceful. They all play a role in the way we experience life.

Q. What is your favourite emotion?

It's important to recognise how we are feeling. Feelings are keys to revealing what we think about things – our mindsets, our belief systems. What we think and subsequently feel, influences the decisions we make and how we live out our life.

THOUGHTS & BELIEFS • FEELINGS • DECISIONS • RESPONSE

All these things influence our behaviours and actions.

Our thoughts and beliefs influence our feelings, which influence our decision-making. These in turn influence our responses to situations.

Feelings should not be ignored or buried. It is not healthy to bottle up all our emotions and it is not healthy to let them take over either. Learning how to identify and acknowledge our feelings will help us deal with emotions in a healthy way.

3. MIRROR EXPLANATION: Our emotions are not wrong, they are an important part of who we are. Our emotions are like a mirror reflecting what is going on inside. Encourage the girls to take some time to look, but be aware that it goes against some cultural traditions. Ask the girls to look into a mirror. What do they see? How we feel does not shape who we are. For example, 'I feel useless, therefore I am useless.' How we are feeling is not joined to our value of self. Understanding what our feelings are telling us helps us to create a balanced and healthy lifestyle.

Spend a few minutes reaffirming the value of feelings, acknowledging the important role they play in our life.

presentation.

GROUP ACTIVITY: IDENTIFYING FEELINGS (see Appendix M)

Who has ever been asked 'How are you?' and your reply was 'I don't know'? Who has ever found themselves crying for no reason? It's important to understand how and why we are feeling this way.

There are four basic feelings each of us has:

FEAR: Fear is a normal emotion. It tells us there may be danger close by. There are times where fear protects us, but there are also times when fear can keep us from moving forward.

HAPPINESS: We enjoy who we are and where we are at when we are happy with life. It's good to sometimes stop and say out loud 'I am happy today!'

ANGER: Our anger is normal and a healthy emotion. It becomes unhealthy when it is used to hurt others (verbal, emotional and physical). There is a big difference between anger and abuse. Anger tells us that there is an issue or a hurt that needs to be resolved.

If we hurt others or others hurt us through anger, seek out professionals or a trusted adult who can help – such as a local GP, counsellor or psychologist.

SADNESS: It's okay to cry. It's natural. It is not a sign of weakness – in fact, it can express how we are feeling when words cannot. It can also release some pressure or stress that we may be feeling. When we find it hard to stop being sad or when we stop doing things we love, then it is important to seek out professional help to assist us to understand why we are feeling sad all the time.

a) Which of the four primary feelings make up the following feelings? Give out cards with different emotions on them. The girls then need to categorise the emotions under the headings: ANGRY, HAPPY, SAD, FEARFUL, COMBINATION.

PRIMARY FEELING	ANGRY	HAPPY	SAD	FEARFUL	COMBINATION
FEELINGS	*Furious*	*Excited*	*Grief*	*Nervous*	*Guilty*
	Irritated	*Satisfied*	*Miserable*	*Terrified*	*Jealous*
	Annoyed	*Pleased*	*Down*	*Anxious*	*Ashamed*
	Ticked off	*Joyful*	*Disappointed*	*Worried*	*Embarrassed*
	Humiliated	*Delighted*	*Hurt*	*Concerned*	*Uncomfortable*
	Frustrated	*Comfortable*	*Lonely*	*Afraid*	*Confused*
	Hurt	*Hopeful*	*Forgotten*	*Uncertain*	*Torn*
	Sarcastic	*Surprised*	*Remorseful*	*Out of control*	*Envious*
	Disgusted	*Positive*	*Rejected*	*Uneasy*	*Compassionate*

b) Feelings Statements: Unpack what feelings can be made up of the combination category.

EG 1:   **STATEMENT: I FEEL EMBARRASSED.**
Q. When you feel embarrassed, are you feeling more sad, fearful or angry?

EG 2:   **STATEMENT: I FEEL DOWN.**
Q. When you feel down, are you feeling more sad, fearful or angry?

Read out feeling statements one at a time and then ask the 'question', encouraging the group to discuss what they feel when hearing the statements. They may feel different emotions to the ones in the 'answer', and that's okay. There are no wrong answers.

We are all unique girls with unique experiences which make up the reasons why we feel certain emotions stronger than others.

GROUP ACTIVITY: ROLE PLAY.
Facilitators to create role plays relevant to their target audience.
Divide the class into groups of 3 or 4. Give each group a different scenario. Each group is to role play the initial reaction they would have in this situation. They are to let their emotions decide for them. Some examples are:

1. The two people who sit behind you in class are always talking. You turn around and tell them to be quiet because you are trying to do your work. The teacher hears you and yells at you to be quiet. She says she is sick of you always distracting the people around you and tells you to stay back after class.

2. You are sitting with all your friends at lunchtime. They start to gossip about a girl who is really quiet and shy. You went to primary school with this girl and know she is really sweet but you don't want your friends to know that you think that.

3. You get home after a long day at school and all you want to do is watch TV for half an hour and have some afternoon tea. As soon as you walk in the door your mum starts nagging you to clean up your room and do your homework.

ACTIVITY: MANAGING OUR EMOTIONS

It's important to maintain a balance when it comes to our emotions and not live a life controlled by them. Our emotions can become like a rollercoaster. If we allow our feelings to get out of balance they can begin to run our lives. In order to keep ourselves balanced we use our emotions to tell us how we are feeling, instead of allowing them to influence our choices in life.

Once we identify our feelings, it may be helpful to explore them further:
- Why am I feeling like this?
- What has caused these feelings?
- What choices do I have?
- Do I need to forgive someone?
- How can I resolve this?
- How long have I felt this way?
- Can I change how I am feeling?

For example: If you're feeling angry, ask yourself:
- 'Why am I angry?'
- 'Where is this coming from?'
- 'What has caused this anger?'
- 'How long has this made me angry?'

When we begin to explore our feelings and the reasons behind them, we start to understand our past and our present and look forward to a different future.

DEMONSTRATION: FIZZY DRINK BOTTLE

When a bottle of fizzy drink is shaken and the lid is taken off, the liquid explodes out of the bottle. Our emotions can do the same thing. They can explode over something that we would normally not get upset over. Our emotions have the potential to dramatically influence all aspects of our life, the choices we make and the kind of relationships we form.

Instead of taking the lid off as soon as you have shaken the fizzy drink bottle, let the bubbles go down for a while before removing the lid. The same goes for our emotions. If possible, leave the room until your emotions calm down and then come back to find a resolution.

Encourage the group to discuss how they keep their emotions balanced in life. Give a personal example. Ask the group for personal examples.

At the end of the day, the greatest thing is that we have the power to choose the life we want.

ACTIVITY: ROLE PLAY
Hand out the "STOP, THINK, CHOOSE" cards using a traffic light example. We DECIDE how we want to behave. Don't let your feelings decide for you, but take your feelings into consideration and use them to your advantage.

After reading the cards ask the girls to redo the role plays with a positive outcome.

PURPOSE: This activity's aim is to slow down the process of making a healthy choice. When we respond to our situations, we are respecting ourselves and others. Respect gives value to ourselves. When we make healthy choices, we place value on ourselves and others.

You can FEEL and then REACT... or...
You can FEEL, STOP, THINK and CHOOSE.
The choice is up to you.

small group discussion.
Q. What did you learn from today's session?
Q. How could you use or apply what you have learnt in your daily life?

ASSESS OUTCOMES
Reinforce the Strength concept. Affirm the group as a whole or to each individual by name 'I have the power of choice.' This exercise is a powerful way to end the session.

shine factor.
IDEAS: Write an encouragement card to each girl, or the girls could write it to somebody else.

note to facilitator.
Set the room up differently today. Create a new mood. Develop a sense of intimacy, connectedness and creative space. One thing you could do is remove the middle table and have the chairs in a circle to create a more intimate atmosphere.

'CHOOSE LIFE'

5
strength.

SESSION FIVE MY DECISIONS DETERMINE MY DESTINATION

MATERIAL REQUIRED: Ball, whiteboard markers, whiteboard, butcher's paper, pens and permanent markers, paper, ribbons, "The ribbon game" handout, name badges, strength quote/affirmation card, bowl

Please see recommended layout below.

ACTIVITY	DETAILS	NOTES/MATERIALS
Icebreaker (5 mins)	Activity: Finish this sentence	RESOURCES: whiteboard
Power Focus (5 mins)	GROUP DISCUSSION: Respect	
Laying The Foundation (15 mins)	ACTIVITIES: Activity: The line game Activity: Convictions Activity: Write a letter	RESOURCES: masking tape, paper.
Presentation (30 mins)	DISCUSSION: Bullying and peer pressure How to be a BIG person DEMONSTRATION: Activity: What's the right choice?	RESOURCES: whiteboard, markers, butcher's paper, permanent markers.
Small Group Discussion (5 mins)	Activity: "The ribbon game" Reinforce Strength concept 'MY DECISIONS DETERMINE MY DESTINATION'	RESOURCES: paper, pens, ribbons, "The ribbon game" handout (See Appendix G).
Shine Factor	As you give out the gifts, encourage each girl	Gifts

outcomes.

By the end of this session, each girl will be able to:

APPLY AND PRACTISE DECISION-MAKING AND PROBLEM-SOLVING SKILLS

IDENTIFY WAYS TO DISPLAY RESPECT TO THEMSELVES AND OTHERS.

icebreaker.
ACTIVITY: FINISH THIS SENTENCE (see Appendix H)
Make this fun and on the light side, not too serious. These can be printed on a handout or written on a whiteboard/poster.

If I could do anything I would like to…

The comic character I would like to be like is…

If I were to write a book it would be…

If I were a musical instrument I would be…

My favourite movie of all time is…

What makes me laugh is…

For alternative icebreakers see Appendix A.

power focus.
STRENGTH COMES IN TWO STAGES:

1. Choice – We hold the power to choose
2. Consequences to our decisions – Decisions determine our destination.

'My decisions determine my destination.'

In every situation, in every day, we make choices. As a result of these choices there are consequences. Consequences will either cause us to move forward in life, stop us from moving at all or cause us to move backwards. There are decisions that can fast track us to our desired destination and others that can keep us from it.

Decisions we make give us control over our life, but they don't just affect our life, they also impact the people around us. Choices can be selfish or selfless.

Every decision we make – from getting out of bed each morning to choosing to arrive at school on time – has a consequence. Our choices impact what our tomorrow will look like. Things we decide to overcome and things we decide to accept all have a direct impact on our life. Often we don't realise that it's the small, everyday decisions that help us move towards our desired destination.

Group Discussion: Respect

Q. Name someone who you look up to and why. This person can be someone you know or a public figure.

Q. How can we respect ourselves?

Q. What does respect look like for you? How would you like people to show you respect?
Starting off with these questions can help the participants understand each other more as well as help them see that how they want to be treated they need to treat others the same.

Q. How can we respect our friends, parents, family, and people from different cultures, religious, racial or linguistic backgrounds? For example, not walking away when your parents are talking to you, listening to someone's story, or experiencing new food and traditions.

Q. What are practical ways you can show respect to your fellow students and teachers?
For example, listening, not speaking over each other, and not talking loudly to someone who speaks with broken English so they don't feel incompetent.

Laying the Foundation

Activity: The Line Game

Mark a line on the floor with tape. Explain that when the facilitator makes a statement or asks a question, the participants need to stand on the line if it applies to them. If it doesn't apply to them, they are to stand off the line. To start the game, the facilitator is to ask questions or make statements that are general and then lead into more specific questions. Lead the specific questions or statements towards respect and bullying. The purpose of this activity is to remove individuals' sense of isolation around this topic and allow everyone to see that respect and bullying applies and impacts everyone in some capacity. Some examples include:

- Stand on the line if you play a sport.
- Stay on the line if you've ever lost a game.
- Stand on the line if you play an instrument or sing.
- Stay on the line if you have ever made a mistake during a performance.
- Stand on the line if you have ever had a bad day at school.
- Stay on the line if you have had more than one bad day at school.
- Stand on the line if you have ever been called names by someone.
- Stay on the line if you have ever had someone try to pick a fight with you.
- Stand on the line if you want bullying to stop.

ACTIVITY: CONVICTIONS

CONVICTION | k*uh* n-vik-sh*uh* n |
A fixed or firm, strong belief.

Convictions are what we believe is important to us. Convictions help us make decisions. Before we make a decision, we can think about whether it is in line with our convictions. There is a reason why we live with convictions. For example, I have a conviction to finish my education pathway because I want to get a good education and set myself up for the future. What are your convictions?

Convictions are formed from our beliefs and values. When we make decisions based on our convictions we are showing others what we believe and value in life.

Having personal convictions will make it easier for us to make the right decisions. Because we believe in our conviction, it gives us strength to act on that decision. Choose friends who have similar values and convictions as you.

Brainstorm the different convictions we have about:
- Family
- Friendships
- Respect
- Money
- Peer pressure
- Role models
- Finishing my education pathway
- Personal characteristics – integrity, honesty, faithfulness
- Achieving dreams.

Put these words in a bowl and ask the girls to pick up a word and share about their conviction on the topic. Make sure there are enough suggestions for everyone.

honour.

HONOUR | *on*-er |
The state of being honoured; the quality of being honourable and having a good name.
Giving worth and weight to what is truly valuable.

At the Olympics, the champions are honoured in front of everyone and presented with medals. At the Golden Globe Awards, the best actor/actress is honoured in front of everyone when receiving their award. In their speeches, they also mention people who they would like to honour for helping them win.

ACTIVITY: WRITE A LETTER
Write a letter to someone in your world who you would like to honour. You may choose to do a drawing instead! It could be for something they have done (for you or generally for others) or for who they are as a person (honest, generous, and faithful). Perhaps it could be a letter to honour your parents by valuing the fact that they brought you into the world. Use coloured paper, permanent markers, and glitter to make it fun and creative!

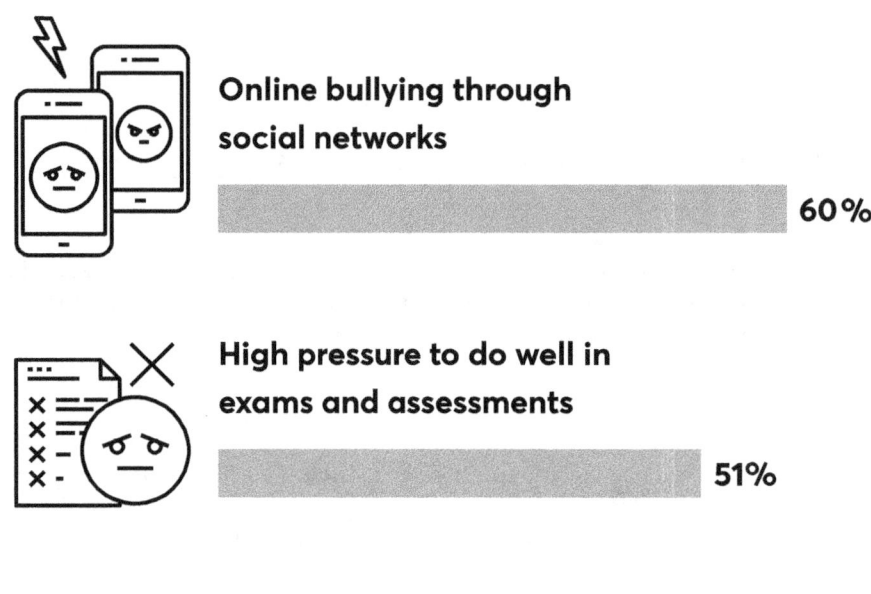

McCrindle (2019), Education Future Forum: Exploring rising parent engagement, the wellbeing focus and school complexity (used with permission).

RESEARCH AND RECORD CURRENT BULLYING STATISTICS RELEVANT TO YOUR GROUP

DISCUSSION: BULLYING

Now that we have identified what respect looks like, what is the opposite of respecting someone? What does that look like?

Bullying is the opposite of respecting others.

Bullying involves intentional acts of harmful behaviour towards another person and normally occurs where there is a power imbalance i.e. where a more powerful person (or people) usurp themselves over another person that they see to be less than. These behaviours include:

- Name-calling
- Physically fighting
- Victimization through ignoring or isolating
- Intimidation and/or harassment, and
- Cyber-bullying

Bullying is not generally a single event of inappropriate behaviour between equals.

Q. A new student has arrived at your school halfway through Term 2. What could you do to help them feel included in a sports lesson?

Cyber-bullying

It is much easier to be more outgoing or provocative online. People find they can be personally more aggressive and forward than they are in 'real-life' because they are hiding behind a computer screen or mobile phone. This can give people the false confidence to say or do things that they would not normally say face-to-face. What they are writing, posting or sending can have a significant negative impact on others.

DISCUSSION: CYBER-BULLYING

Q. What are some types of cyber-bullying?

Encourage the participants to come up with their thoughts. Then suggest some of the following forms if they have been left out. Forms of cyber-bullying include:
- Spreading rumours about people on social media, via text messages or online
- Accessing another person's account information, without permission, to see their details or to pretend to be them
- Sexting unsolicited photos or messages
- Trolling

Q. What effect do you think cyber-bullying has on the recipient and the cyber-bullies?

Encourage the participants to come up with their thoughts. Then suggest some of the following forms if they have been left out:
- It can have a plethora of negative effects on the recipient
- Once circulated on the internet, it may never disappear. Info and images can be found at later times
- What is posted online may have a negative effect on future applications for college or employment
- Cyber-bullies may face legal charges. e.g. if the cyber-bullying is sexual in nature such as sexting

Q. What can you do to help prevent cyber-bulling?
- Avoid getting involved in it yourself
- Avoid forwarding bullying texts and emails and exit online chat rooms
- Block the sender
- Ignore the message rather than respond in a manner that would encourage retaliation
- Think about how you can respond as a helpful bystander
- Request removal of objectionable websites.

ACTIVITY: WHAT'S THE RIGHT CHOICE?

Present the following scenario to your Shine group.

SCENARIO

During lunch you see two of your friends having a massive fight on the oval. A large group of students are watching. Select the right response:

A Look the other way and continue walking. Your friends have had fights in the past and they have always been fine afterwards. It's okay to do nothing.

B Join the other students and watch. The fight will be the talk of the school tomorrow and you will need to see what happened to join in with the gossip. This is the right choice.

C Get a staff member immediately. The teacher/support staff will be able to help stop the fight and help your friends if they are hurt. Your friends might get into trouble, but this is the right thing for you to do *(correct response)*.

D Stop and record the fight on your mobile phone. The right thing to do is to post the video onto social media and see how many 'likes' you can get.

Discuss each response with your ShineGIRL group. Once your group has selected the correct response discuss with them how by getting a staff member immediately, they would be helping to create a safe and supportive school community.

small group discussion.

ACTIVITY: THE RIBBON GAME

Provide the girls with The Ribbon Game handout (see Appendix G) and discuss as a group. Ask the girls to select a piece of ribbon that best describes them (ensure you have enough of each colour ribbon for each girl to select the same one – sometimes this does happen!). The girls can take their ribbon home with them.

ASSESS OUTCOMES

Reinforce the Strength concept. Declare to the group as a whole or tell each individual by name, 'My decisions determine my destination'.

shine factor.

IDEAS: Strength quote and affirmation card.

'CHOOSE LIFE'

strength.

SESSION SIX | HAVE RESILIENCE

MATERIAL REQUIRED:
Chopsticks, jelly beans, bowls, paper, coloured pens/pencils, ball, whiteboard markers

Please see recommended layout below.

ACTIVITY	DETAILS	NOTES/MATERIALS
Icebreaker (5 mins)	Activity: Chopsticks game	RESOURCES: chopsticks, jelly beans, bowls
Power Focus (5 mins)	Group Discussion: What does resilience look like to you?	
Foundational Concept (10 mins)	RESILIENCE	
Presentation (30 mins)	Demonstration: Movie Scene Group Discussion: Resilience in young people Activity: Personal reflection	RESOURCES: ball
Small Group Discussion (10 mins)	Q. What have you learnt today that you can practically apply to your life now?	
Shine Factor	As you give out the gifts, encourage each girl	Gifts

outcomes.
By the end of this session, each girl will be able to:

RECOGNISE THE VALUE OF DEVELOPING RESILIENCE.

icebreaker.
ACTIVITY: CHOPSTICKS GAME

Split the group up into their teams. Give each student a bowl with some jellybeans in it and a set of chopsticks. No one is to eat the jellybeans until the game starts. Explain the instructions of the game; each participant has to try and eat the jelly beans using chopsticks ONLY – NO HANDS.

This game will take some time for the participants to finish and will test their patience, willpower and resilience. Take note of the different reactions everyone has to the game. This activity may bring many things to the surface to talk about during group discussion. Keep an eye out for participants that lose their patience and give up and participants that persevered through the game until they ate all their jelly beans. The team that finishes first wins.

power focus.

Get into small groups and discuss what you believe resilience is and what it looks like to the girls. Then bring the group back as a whole and write answers on the whiteboard, encouraging the girls that there are no wrong answers, as it could be individual to the person.

laying the foundation.

RESILIENCE | ri-zil-ee-*uh* ns |

The ability to recover readily from adversity.

RESILIENCE

Resilience is the strength to withstand adversity. It is the ability to handle difficult situations, people, environments and setbacks. Being able to bounce back and recover from adversity makes us stronger and contributes to our dreams becoming a reality. Young people can have incredible resilience. They can continually surprise us with their ability to bounce back rather than giving in to circumstances.

A resilient person is able to stand firm whilst facing significant difficulties and stress, as they have a strong sense of self-belief and faith in their capabilities.

We need to understand that life will not always be smooth sailing. Life is not always great. Things happen that we would prefer didn't. But if life was always wonderful, would we appreciate all the great things or would we take them for granted? We can learn so much about ourselves when we go through challenges and problems. It is never comfortable when you're in the middle of adversity or challenge, but when you get through it you can look back and see what you have learnt from the situation. Any mistakes we make are simply an opportunity to grow and learn.

presentation.

DEMONSTRATION: MOVIE SCENE
Choose a movie that displays a character that has overcome adversity and developed resilience. Show a few scenes that display their experience of adversity and resilience to explain this concept further. Suggested movies that relate to resilience include The Pursuit of Happiness, The Blind Side, and Racing Stripes.

GROUP DISCUSSION: RESILIENCE IN YOUNG PEOPLE
Q. What are some challenges young people face every day?
- Peer pressure
- Losing a loved one/family breakdown
- Bullying
- Rejection
- Negative self-talk
- Loneliness
- Addictions and substance use

Q. How can you increase your resilience?
- Healthy relationships
- Not taking things personally
- Participation
- Learning from your failures
- Communication (someone to talk to)
- Getting information to understand what you're facing
- Overcoming problems, not giving up
- Adapting to new situations easily
- Standing up for what you believe
- Being honest about your fears
- Taking healthy risks
- Figuring out who you are and what you want out of life, and not giving up on it
- Facing rejection or setbacks and trying again
- Persevering no matter what
- Spending time with people who handle stress well.

Q. What can make it harder to overcome?
- Isolation
- Negativity
- Boredom
- Indifference

'Start believing in what you can offer.'

ACTIVITY: PERSONAL REFLECTION

OPTION I: Distribute a piece of paper and pen for each individual. On one side of the paper write down 'Where I have persevered' and on the other side of the paper write down 'Where I have given up'. Encourage the group to spend some time writing down their personal answers.

OR

OPTION II: Write down a list of positive achievements you have accomplished and a list of difficult experiences you have overcome or survived. After they have done this, bring the class back together and ask if anyone wants to share what they have written. Explore what participants gained from persevering, and if anything was gained from giving up.

Use this to build and encourage the group to stay motivated when facing difficult situations. As the facilitator, be prepared to start the discussion off first.

Encourage the group that if and when they face tough challenges in their life, it's important to talk about it with someone they trust. Planning and problem-solving challenges can help us overcome. We can't do life alone. We need each other.

small group discussion.

Q. What have you learnt today that you can practically apply to your life now?

shine factor.

Have the words relating to Strength already written out on a smooth stone.

note to the facilitator.

Remember every participant's response is always valid – never shame a person for their answer and always look for the positive.

'I HAVE A HOPE AND A FUTURE'

P
purpose.

SESSION SEVEN MY POTENTIAL IS LIMITLESS
SESSION EIGHT MY LIFE HAS PURPOSE
SESSION NINE SHINE!

BASIS. 'I HAVE A HOPE AND A FUTURE.'

introduction.

The torment of purposelessness can tear a person apart. As Archbishop Desmond Tutu says, 'We humans can tolerate suffering but we cannot tolerate meaninglessness.'

Everyone yearns to live a life that is significant. We often go through the motions of life getting caught up in the busyness, which can cause us to neglect our purpose; the 'something' we are passionate about that lies inside each and every one of us.

'Our passions are what make our heart sing.'

Our passions are linked to and help us identify and complete our purpose; what we were created for. As we begin to discover and live our life with purpose, we become less discouraged about where we are heading in life. We were not created to live our lives alone. We need friends who help prepare us for the challenges ahead and who are committed to walk through them with us. Nothing can substitute friendships and interpersonal communication. Gathering together with like-minded people who spur us on and encourage us to not give up on our dreams helps us when we are feeling disheartened or discouraged. We can start discovering our purpose now.

'Don't despise the days of small beginnings!'

THE PURPOSE CONCEPT EXPLORES:

my potential is
LIMITLESS.

Potential is what we are capable of becoming in every area of our life. This can include friends, family, career, health, finances, personal character and attitude. Our potential is limitless. Our potential is often in seed form. The seeds inside us are limitless. Each seed has the potential to grow and become everything it was designed to be. The only thing that can limit us from becoming all that we can be is <u>us</u>. Living in our potential requires believing in ourselves and being confident in who we are. Our potential will not grow or be realised unless we choose to put it into action.

What do you believe about yourself?

my life has PURPOSE.

We are unique; there is no one else like us. How we are designed, our passions, our talents, and our strengths are unique to each of us and have purpose. There is a blueprint inside all of us. We are purpose-built and exist for a reason. There is a purpose for our life.

Discovering our purpose is a key aspect to every person's journey. We get a taste of our purpose when we tap into the desires of our heart. What satisfies us and what makes us frustrated? We each have a specific wiring with a palette of gifts and strengths that are as unique to each individual as a thumbprint!

Developing our gifts and talents, identifying our dreams and desires and learning how to use them, all help us to live a life of purpose. Purpose enables us to make a difference in our world. Life does not have to be about just living for ourselves. Our life can be used to make a difference for others.

We can choose to live in a world that is about ourselves or we can choose to include others in our world where we can make a difference.

**KEY MESSAGE TO REINFORCE
THROUGH PURPOSE SESSIONS**

*my potential is limitless!
my life has purpose!*

'I HAVE A HOPE AND A FUTURE'

purpose.

SESSION SEVEN MY POTENTIAL IS LIMITLESS

MATERIAL REQUIRED: Potting mix, polystyrene cups, water, walkway, music, apple seeds, name badges, whiteboard markers, whiteboard pens, coloured pencils, permanent markers, paper

Please see recommended layout below.

ACTIVITY	DETAILS	NOTES/MATERIALS
Icebreaker (5 mins)	Activity: Walking tall	RESOURCES: a walkway, appropriate upbeat music.
Power Focus (10 mins)	'MY POTENTIAL IS LIMITLESS'	RESOURCES: apple seed
Foundational Concept (10 mins)	Group Discussion: Seeds of greatness	RESOURCES: whiteboard, whiteboard marker.
Presentation (30 mins)	Activity: Planting a seed Choosing confidence	RESOURCES: potting mix, seed, water, cup, walkway, music.
Small Group Discussion (5 mins)	Q. What can you do with these seeds starting today? Reinforce Purpose concept 'MY POTENTIAL IS LIMITLESS'	
Shine Factor	As you give out the gifts, encourage each girl	Gifts

outcomes.
By the end of this session, each girl will be able to:

RECOGNISE THE VALUE OF A POSITIVE ENVIRONMENT FOR HER POTENTIAL TO GROW

IDENTIFY WAYS TO BUILD HER CONFIDENCE.

icebreaker.
ACTIVITY: WALKING TALL

Invite the group to stand and encourage each one to participate in the following exercise.

Close your eyes and imagine that you are walking towards your dreams. By doing something different, we are learning more about us – our limits and our capabilities. We are expanding our capacity to meet challenges head on. Only have one girl at a time walking tall on the walkway.

When the girls get to the end of the walkway, encourage them to declare 'My potential is limitless'.

The rest of the group is the encouraging cheer squad applauding each girl.

STEPS TO WALKING TALL

Step 1: Breathe in deeply through your nose until you feel your stomach and diaphragm swell. Now slowly contract your stomach from your pelvis to your rib cage and breathe slowly out through your mouth.

Step 2: Hold your shoulders back, tighten your bottom and straighten your back. Now look straight ahead at eye level so that your head is evenly poised above the spine and is at a right angle position to your neck.

power focus.
'MY POTENTIAL IS LIMITLESS'

What is potential?

POTENTIAL
| p*uh*-ten-sh*uh* l |
Possible, capable of being or becoming.

Potential is what we are capable of becoming in every area of our life. This can include friends, family, career, health, finances, personal character and attitude.

Our potential is limitless. Our potential is often in seed form. The seeds inside us are limitless. Each seed has potential to grow and become everything it was designed to be.

The only thing that can limit us from becoming all that we can be is us.

Living in our potential requires believing in ourselves and being confident in who we are.
Our potential will not grow or be realised unless we choose to put action to it.

"Your potential is really up to you. It doesn't matter what others might think. It doesn't matter where you came from. It doesn't even matter what you might have believed about yourself at a previous time in your life. It's about what lies within you and whether you can bring it out."

JOHN C. MAXWELL
Talent is Never Enough (pg 18)

laying the foundation.

GROUP DISCUSSION: SEEDS OF GREATNESS

PLANTING A SEED

Ask the girls to place their names on their cup. Then place a little bit of potting mix inside, plant the seed, add more potting mix and then water.

1. Each girl has their planted seed in front of them. Even though they can't see the seed, it is planted inside their cup. Often in life, if we can't see our potential, we consequently overlook it – 'There is no seed in here', 'I have no potential.' Just because we can't see the seed doesn't mean it isn't within us and it isn't growing. We need to believe in our potential!

2. Hold up a tiny apple seed for the group to see. This seed has the potential to be an orchard. A seed produces an apple tree, which produces apples, which produce more seeds. These seeds produce more apple trees, apples and seeds. The growth is ongoing.

Seeds have so much potential. Our purpose cannot grow unless we first recognise we have seeds of potential within us.

'Everything that we need to live the life we want is already planted inside us.'

Q. How do we look after our seeds of greatness?
- We nurture the seeds by valuing ourselves.
- Create the right environment to bring forth the life we want – surround ourselves with healthy relationships, positive role models, and encouraging people.
- Being positive and believing in our potential.
- Giving ourselves opportunity to develop and try new things.
- Keeping our health in balance – physically, emotionally, mentally, spiritually.
- We can live our life as a garden. What grows is what we plant, and what we let others plant in it. We can choose what seeds we plant in our own garden. Seeds can be skills, knowledge, experiences, thoughts and ideas.

presentation.
ACTIVITY: CHOOSING CONFIDENCE
Q. Where is our confidence found?
Q. Are we born with it?

Confidence comes from embracing who we are. To live in our potential sometimes requires us to step out of our comfort zone and do new things. How confident we grow is our choice. A key to living in our potential is choosing to believe in ourselves and be confident. To get something we don't have, sometimes we need to do something we haven't done before.

Q. What are some things that can hinder you from growing in your potential?
Q. Is there something standing in your way from moving toward growing the seed that is within you?

CONFIDENCE | kon-fi-d*uh* ns l |
Full trust: belief in the trustworthiness or reliability of a person or thing, boldness, self-assurance and poise.

Write that obstacle on a piece of paper. Now close your eyes and think about achieving your potential and envision yourself moving toward growing that seed. Don't allow any negative thoughts to come in and distract you from achieving that potential.

After you have seen yourself reaching your potential and nurturing that seed of greatness, take that piece of paper, crumple it up and walk confidently down the walkway and throw it in the bin. You can even have the girls declare 'My potential is limitless!' at the end.

discussion and wrap-up.

Q. What can you do with these seeds starting today? Share with the group.

ASSESS OUTCOMES
Reinforce Purpose concept. Affirm the group as a whole or to each individual by name, 'My potential is limitless'. This exercise is a powerful way to end the session.

shine factor.
IDEAS: A bag of seeds, a juicy apple, 'seeds of greatness' quote. (See Appendix I)

note to facilitator.
This can be a very powerful exercise. Keep the atmosphere light-hearted and fun. Ensure you have some good music. Look out for girls who may need extra care and encouragement.

'I HAVE A HOPE AND A FUTURE'

purpose.

SESSION EIGHT MY LIFE HAS PURPOSE

MATERIAL REQUIRED: Wrapping paper and colourful ribbon, cardboard – 1 sheet per girl, example of a dream collage, IMAGINE handout, crayons, permanent markers, stickers, glitter, scissors, glue, magazines or magazine cut-outs, 'My life has purpose' worksheet

Please see recommended layout below.

ACTIVITY	DETAILS	NOTES/MATERIALS
Icebreaker (5 mins)	Activity: Wrap Up A Gift	RESOURCES: wrapping material
Power Focus (5 mins)	'MY LIFE HAS PURPOSE'	
Laying The Foundation (15 mins)	What is your heart song? What is your life's blueprint?	
Presentation (30 mins)	Activity: Dream collage	RESOURCES: paper, pens, collage materials, newspaper, sticky tape, IMAGINE handout (see Appendix J).
Small Group Discussion (5 mins)	Questions about how to live your dreams. Reinforce Purpose concept 'MY LIFE HAS PURPOSE'	
Shine Factor	As you give out the gifts, encourage each girl	Gifts

outcomes.
By the end of this session, each girl will be able to:
IDENTIFY PERSONAL DESIRES
DEVELOP AN UNDERSTANDING THAT SHE HAS SOMETHING TO CONTRIBUTE.

icebreaker.
ACTIVITY: WRAP UP A GIFT

Have each girl wrap a small gift with 'love' for someone else. Give them materials to wrap and decorate the gift. As the gift is for someone else, encourage them to make the gift special.

PURPOSE: 'Our life is a gift'. Our life is designed to be a gift to others. Our smile, our love, our care and kind words are a gift to people around us. We are valuable. This gives us a new spin on life. Living is not just about getting through the day-to-day activities; it is also about those moments that fill our heart with joy and gladness. We can contribute to the world around us.

power focus.
"MY LIFE HAS PURPOSE."

We are unique; there is no one else like us. How we are designed, our passions, our talents, and our strengths are unique to each of us and have purpose. All these qualities are in us so that we can fulfil our personal desires. There is a blueprint inside all of us. We are purpose-built and exist for a reason. There is a purpose for our life.

Discovering our purpose is a key aspect to every person's journey. We get a taste of our purpose when we tap into the desires of our heart. What satisfies us and what makes us frustrated? We each have a specific wiring with a palette of gifts and strengths that are as unique to each individual as a thumbprint!

Developing our gifts and talents, identifying our dreams and desires and learning how to use them, all help us to live a life of purpose. Purpose enables us to make a difference in our world. Life does not have to be about just living for ourselves. Our life can be used to make a difference for others.

We can choose to live in a world that is about ourselves
or we can choose to include others in our world and make a difference.

laying the foundation.

Q. What is your heart song?
The world we live in can try to label us, put titles on us and make us try and fit into a certain box, telling us 'This is the way to be significant, popular or successful'.

In the movie Happy Feet, young Mumble's song was not singing, but tap dancing. This is what he was born to do, yet his behaviour was 'un-penguin' like. We all have a song to sing. We all have a message over our life, a reason for our existence, and a purpose to our life.

What melody does your heart sing? What flows naturally from your life?

By being true to ourselves, we can find our heart song and use it to create a difference in the world. In turn, others have the choice to do the same. Suggest the girls watch the movie Happy Feet as an example of a heart song, on their own time.

Discovering our purpose is challenging on its own and can get harder when family and friends have expectations of us. Our desires and dreams may be different to what they want. As we journey into teenage life and adulthood, it's important to find out what is right for us and the life we want, while still honouring our family.

Part of our journey into becoming a woman is discovering how to balance honouring our families, as well as ourselves, and our own personal journey that is unique to each of us!

OPTIONAL DISCUSSION QUESTIONS:
- What does honouring yourself look like for you?
- How can we honour our parents but still stay on course to reach our dreams?
- How do our parents feel when we show them respect?
- How would you like to be shown respect?

presentation.
ACTIVITY: DREAM COLLAGE

This activity is about each girl creatively expressing their dreams and desires for their future through creating a 'dream' collage. This activity is significant, as it gives girls the opportunity to dream big for their future. A visual representation of one's hopes and dreams is a powerful message that can inspire, strengthen and encourage us in our personal journey of purpose and significance. The activity is also a great technique for girls to begin their discovery of how unique they are.

Write on the board:

If money, time, place, ability, education and confidence were not an issue, what would you do with your life? (If you knew you could not fail, what would you do?)

- Distribute to each girl a piece of cardboard and ask them to write their name in the centre.
- Distribute magazines, scissors, glue and pens.
- Show the girls an example collage.
- Give the participants license to dream, imagine, reflect and create what they desire.
- Encourage the girls to imagine the paper as a blank canvas (see Appendix J for the IMAGINE handout).

Words and images both contribute to a strong statement about their life dreams. Laminate collages once completed if the girls desire. When they are finished, ask a few of the girls (all girls, if time permits) to present their collage to the rest of the group. Encourage them to find a special place to hang their collage where they can see it and be inspired to go for it!

Explore the thoughts on the following page before attempting the dream collage [22]

IMAGINE

BIRTHDAY SPEECHES

Imagine it is your birthday. What would you like people to say about you for your birthday speech? What would you like people to write about you on your birthday card?

LIKES

If you had the total approval and admiration of everyone, regardless of what you do, what would you do with your life?

ROLE MODELS

What role models do you look up to? Who inspires you? What personal strengths or qualities do they have that you admire?

CHARACTER STRENGTHS

What personal strengths and qualities do you already have? Which ones would you like to develop? How would you like to apply them?

WEALTH

Imagine you win the lottery or inherit a fortune. How would you spend it? Who would you share it with?

watch out for DREAM STEALERS!

FEAR

SELF-DOUBT

NEGATIVE COMMENTS

BAD CIRCUMSTANCES

LACK OF CONFIDENCE

DRUGS OR ALCOHOL

DISTRACTION

BULLYING

PEER PRESSURE

BELIEVING THAT OTHER THINGS ARE MORE IMPORTANT THAN YOU

small group discussion.
Q. Ask the girls to share their collage with the group and discuss.

shine factor.
Each girl is to take their gift and turn to the person next to them. They are to exchange gifts. They should be encouraged to place value on the other person, and speak from their heart – with love – as they give the gift. Make sure they take turns – not simultaneously!!

note to facilitator.
This is a big session with a lot to fit in and every part is important. Be well prepared and keep it to the timeframe. Be aware that some girls may not be aware of any hopes or dreams for their future. Perhaps have one of your team sit with the girls during the collage activity and give prompts through noticing what they are interested in and asking questions based on the collage shield. Keep the collages and present them to the girls next week.

'I HAVE A HOPE AND A FUTURE'

9

purpose.

SESSION NINE SHINE!

MATERIAL REQUIRED: Arrangements organised for outing including transport and any permissions required, Shine Factor personalised message for each girl, Celebrating the Shine journey handout (see Appendix L), Certificates

Please see recommended layout below.

ACTIVITY	DETAILS	NOTES/MATERIALS
Icebreaker (5 mins)	Activity: Personal testimonies	
Presentation (50 mins)	OPTIONS: (choose between) Movie night Special outing Pass the 'ShineGIRL' message on to others	
Small Group Discussion (5 mins)	Ask the girls to share what they have leant from ShineGIRL and how they can pass on what they have learnt to others.	
Shine Factor	As you give out the gifts, encourage each girl	Gifts

outcomes.
By the end of this session, each girl will be able to:
DESCRIBE WHAT SHE HAS LEARNT.

icebreaker.
ACTIVITY: PERSONAL TESTIMONIES
Ask the girls to share what they think their purpose may be or encourage the girls to share what they have learnt from ShineGIRL.

presentation.
HERE ARE 3 OPTIONS TO CHOOSE BETWEEN:
1. Plan an outing in advance to a swish hotel or restaurant to treat the girls to a special time. This could be coffee and dessert, a light supper or whatever you are able to do. Maybe you can create a special room with a WOW factor for the girls. Whatever it is, it'll be a great surprise for the girls.

This week is an opportunity to apply the skills, knowledge and attitudes gained throughout the message as the group is taken on a significant and special outing. This could be a special restaurant, a classy café for hot chocolate and cake, or a special lunch put on by a local girl's group. For some girls this is often the first time that a confident and positive sense of self is required.

Here are some things for you to consider and organise in order to make this trip a success:

TRANSPORT – Chartered bus, public transport or choose a location within walking distance.

PERMISSION – A school authorisation to take the participants off school grounds. Where an activity is run with students from a school, a school staff member(s) will normally be required to lead the excursion. Parental authorisation (permission notes need to be made up and distributed by the school contact; ask a teacher for guidelines as to what information is required on the note, however, the school usually organises this). A school authorisation for extra time (this outing might require more time than one school period).

COST – Try and keep the cost for each individual under $10.

2. Hold a movie night at a special room at the school. Choose a movie that is uplifting and inspirational. Create the atmosphere with candles, cushions and throw rugs. Design a menu with a choice of beverages and light snacks (see Appendix K for a sample). Suggested movies that relate to living life with purpose: Amazing Grace, Forrest Gump, Coach Carter, Freedom Writers.
    * Check movie classifications to make sure it is suitable for the age of the girls

    Or take the time to view (and maybe take action in) social justice exploits:
    - Girleffect.org
    - Iheartrevolution.org
    - Halftheskymovement.org

3. Explore and discuss with the group what they have learnt from ShineGIRL and how they can pass on what they have learnt to others. Some suggestions include: Write (and create) an encouragement card to someone in difficult circumstances. Spend quality time with someone in a hospital or nursing home. Write a thank you card to someone for their life and contribution they have made to the community. Plan a justice project. A justice project is about creating a special experience for someone else. As a group, organise to do something beyond yourselves to make a difference in someone else's life. For example, an excursion to visit some homeless people or shelter, correctional facility, nursing home, put together a food basket, bake a cake for a next door neighbour, or visit a non-for-profit organisation like Mission Australia or World Vision.

celebration and presentation of certificates.

At this time all the girls will be seated. This celebration gives the opportunity for each girl to stand up, receive her certificate and declare statements about herself. There is power in speaking out loud.

Q. What do you stand for or what kind of declaration would you like to make over your life?
- I am valuable
- My decisions determine my destination
- I am one-of-a-kind
- I have resilience
- I am wonderfully made
- My potential is limitless
- I have the power of choice
- My life has purpose

ASSESS OUTCOMES
Encourage the girls to stay connected and build on the networks they have made during the group if possible.

shine factor.
IDEAS: The Shine scroll found in Appendix L or a handmade bracelet with beads. If you can find alphabet beads, have the word "shine" as part of the bracelet.

note to facilitator.
See Appendix L for an example of a certificate.

NOTES

A
appendices.

SHINEGIRL MATERIALS

A. ALTERNATIVE ICEBREAKERS
B. THE QUESTIONNAIRE GAME
C. INTERESTING FACTS ABOUT HANDS
D. HAIR CARE SUGGESTIONS
E. A TEACUP STORY
F. I HAVE THE POWER OF CHOICE
G. THE RIBBON GAME
H. FINISH THE SENTENCE
I. SEEDS OF GREATNESS
J. IMAGINE
K. CELEBRATION SAMPLE MENU
L. SHINE SCROLL & CERTIFICATE
M. FEELING CARDS
N. ADDITIONAL ACTIVITIES

NOTES

APPENDIX A - ALTERNATIVE ICEBREAKERS

Icebreakers appeal to all 3 key learning styles; learning by seeing, learning by experiencing for oneself and learning by hearing. This keeps participants involved. ICEBREAKERS ARE FUN! They increase both the capacity to take in information and the retention of knowledge. Icebreakers are interactive. Participants immediately feel involved and part of the group. This allows the group to feel relaxed and begin to bond.

REMEMBER: NEVER FORCE ANYONE TO PARTICIPATE!

The following are examples only. Feel free to be creative and adapt activities to best fit for your particular group.

1. PASS THE MYSTERY BOX

In an ornate medium-sized box, place easy-to-read cards with individual non-confronting questions. The box is randomly given to the first person and she selects a question like 'favourite food', answers it and then passes the box to the next girl along. If the girl is unable to think of an answer she can pass but the box must come back to her at the end for another go (as long as this person wants to participate). BENEFITS: Aids communication, team-building, and group bonding.

2. WHISPERS

Using a message (which may be relevant to the day's shine session) whisper to the first person the message. They then whisper the message to the next person and so on until the last person has heard the message. They then announce what was said in the original message. No repeats are allowed along the way. The message is quite different to the way it started out! Talk a little about communication and its importance. BENEFITS: Communication skills, team-building, group bonding and comfort zones.

3. IF I WERE A PAINTER

Finish the sentence 'If I were a painter, I would paint a picture of...?' BENEFITS: Communication skills, team-building, aids self-awareness

APPENDIX A - ALTERNATIVE ICEBREAKERS

4. BAKE THE CAKE

With a large mixing bowl in the middle of the table (it can be pretend) each person has on a card an ingredient that makes up the basic cake mixture. Facilitators read out the instructions and each person with the ingredient card has to complete the action.

125 grams butter
1 cup of sugar
5 ml vanilla
2 eggs
2 cups of self-raising flour
¼ cup of milk
Pinch of salt

METHOD
- Place butter and sugar in large mixing bowl and beat until creamy.
- Add vanilla and mix.
- Add eggs and mix well until mixture is an even texture.
- Sift flour and salt into mixture and blend.
- Add milk to mixture after first cup of flour and blend to an even consistency.

At the end, comment on the fun and team work. This is a real recipe for cupcakes. (Use real ingredients if you're game!) You may wish to give out the recipe on a laminated card as a Shine Factor. BENEFITS: Communication skills, team building, fun!

5. PASS THE PARCEL

Using funky, up-beat music, pass a box around the group with treats in it. When the music stops, the person can select an item out of the box. Others in the group aren't allowed to see what's in the box until it's their turn. At the end when everyone has something from the box, go around the group and ask why they chose this. You may have left over Shine Factors or laminated quotes or something completely random like toys. They can either be kept or returned. It's up to you how you use it. BENEFITS: Self-awareness (what I like), team-building, fun!

APPENDIX A - ALTERNATIVE ICEBREAKERS

6. GIFT EXCHANGE
Using your Shine Factor for the day, set out the table with enough gifts for everyone (it works best if it's the same gift). Have sufficient wrapping paper/tissue paper, scissors and tape for the group to wrap one item each. Add ribbon and anything else creative like stickers, flowers and so forth. Show the group 'How To' wrap a gift and then add ribbon and a touch of creativity to inspire theirs. Curling ribbon or adding 2 colours together can be fun. BENEFITS: Self-awareness (what I like), team-building, creativity, relaxing, fun!

7. WHAT'S MISSING?
Grab a number of items (10 is good) and place them in a line on a table in front of you (it can be anything you have, but ensure it is non-imposing). You can use grocery items (a packet of soup, toothpaste, a tin of tuna and so forth). Go through the items and ask the group to remember what is there. Either have the group close their eyes or cover and remove a number of items (Start with 2 and make it harder by taking more items or by shifting them around). Have the group identify 'what's missing'. BENEFITS: Awareness, mind workout, group participation.

8. GETTING TO KNOW YOU.
This exercise is great to use when you are aware of the dynamics of your group, and they like to chat, as it encourages open sharing. Give permission for anyone to pass. Ask each person to share something that they have learnt since the group has started. What have they gleaned or what has inspired them? Or simply recap what we did last week! BENEFITS: Opens communication, self-awareness, group bonding, peer awareness.

9. FINISH THIS SENTENCE
Using sentence completion allows each person to share something about them in a 'safe' way. Make this fun and on the light side, not too serious. These can be put on a handout or on a whiteboard/poster:
- If I could do anything I would like to…
- The comic character I would like to be like is…
- If I were to write a book it would be…
- If I were a musical instrument I would be…
- My favourite movie of all time is…
- What makes me laugh is…

BENEFITS: Opens communication, self-awareness, group bonding, peer awareness, fun!

APPENDIX A - ALTERNATIVE ICEBREAKERS

10. TRUSTING DRIVERS
Pair up! Set up an obstacle course. Participants stand behind their partner and "drive" their partner, who has their eyes shut, around the room as fast and as safely as they can. This can be down as a wheelbarrow race, on skateboards, etc. as long as it is safe! BENEFITS: Communication skills, energetic, fun!

11. HEAVY HANDS
Get the group to shut their eyes and imagine a helium balloon attached to one hand and a very heavy book resting in the other. With the help of a few simple suggestions, participants' subconscious minds react as if opposing forces were real and one hand feels like it's getting heavier. BENEFITS: Demonstration of power of suggestion vs. reality, interesting.

12. GREETINGS
Provide either blank cards or have the group create a card with an envelope. Ask the group to think of someone they would like to give the card to and write something special on the inside. Provide stamps if needed. BENEFITS: Communication, creativity, promotes generosity.

13. 2 TRUTHS AND A LIE
Each person tells three things about themselves: two true and one not true. The group tries to guess which is not true. BENEFITS: Communication, fun!

14. JOURNALIST
Get into pairs or small groups and find out about the other person/s. This does not have to be personal – it can be your likes, sports, crafts, foods etc. (they may write down the details or not). Swap over and the other person asks questions. BENEFITS: Communication, self/others awareness, bonding, fun

15. THANK YOU CARD
Have the group make a thank you card for someone – be as creative as time and budget allow. BENEFITS: Communication, thankfulness, creativity.

APPENDIX A - ALTERNATIVE ICEBREAKERS

16. A FEW OF MY FAVOURITE THINGS
In your journal, get the group to work on a list of at least 10 favourite things. This can be anything;, people, places, foods. Once completed, get the group to share on these things. BENEFITS: Positivity, awareness.

17. NEWSPAPER DRESS-UP GAME
Each group decides on a scenario for their perfect date. They choose one person in the group to be the model and using newspaper have to create the perfect outfit. Give the girls a time limit. They then parade the outfit in a fashion show for the rest of the class. Another person in the group describes the outfit.

18. TUG-O-WAR
Ask the class who the strongest person in the room is. Then ask who isn't very strong and has trouble lifting heavy things. Explain to the girls that we are going to have a game of tug-o-war and the strongest person is going to be playing against 4 of the people who said they are weak. Hopefully the team of weaker people will win. Explain that strength is not about being independent and being able to do everything on our own; it's about being able to work well with other people. We are stronger when we draw on one another's strengths. We can achieve so much more in a group than we can on our own.

19. BLIND MAZE
In the classroom, set up an obstacle course using chairs, bags etc. Be aware of sharp corners or anything that could cause someone to trip over. The girls need to get into pairs. In each pair, one girl needs to be blindfolded and the other girl is the guide. The guide is not allowed to touch the blindfolded girls but has to talk her through the obstacle course and lead her to the end.

APPENDIX B - THE QUESTIONNAIRE GAME

the questionnaire game.

YOUR NAME	YOUR NAME
YOUR BIRTHDAY	YOUR BIRTHDAY

YOUR FAVOURITE:

Song

Colour

Movie

Animal

Shop

Thing to do

Subject

Drink

TV show

Food

Sport

Job

Holiday

YOUR FAVOURITE:

Song

Colour

Movie

Animal

Shop

Thing to do

Subject

Drink

TV show

Food

Sport

Job

Holiday

APPENDIX C - INTERESTING FACTS ABOUT HANDS

interesting facts about.
HANDS.

each hand contains...
- 29 major and minor bones.
- At least 123 named ligaments.
- 34 muscles that move the fingers and thumb.
- 48 nerves and 30 named arteries.
- A quarter of the part of the brain that controls movement in the body is devoted to the muscles of the hands.
- There are no muscles in your fingers. The muscles that move your fingers are located in the palm and up in the forearm.
- Your fingernails grow about the same amount as the continents move every year.
- It takes 6 months for your fingernails to grow all the way from the root to tip, and structurally, fingernails are modified hairs.
- Everyone has unique patterns on their palms and fingertips. The palm of your hands and the soles of your feet have the thickest skin of the human body.
- Our palms are hairless and don't tan. While being tough and durable, our hands are very sensitive.

hands are expressive and creative.
- They touch: one of the 5 senses
- They massage, stroke, caress
- They speak emotion: happiness, anger, nervousness, excitement.
- They grasp and embrace
- They pull and push
- They guide and point
- They can tell a story: weathered, tanned, rough, calloused, manicured, wrinkled, soft, dry.

hands in action.
- A handshake
- A helping hand
- A soothing hand
- A hand up and a hand out
- A hand of friendship
- A hand extends to the poor and to the needy
- Creation: they make/cook and creativity: music/art, etc
- They bring gifts to people.

The single most important thing we can do to keep from getting sick and spreading illness is to clean our hands. Think about touching tables, doorknobs, desks and telephones; bacteria from hands can survive from 20 mins – 2 hrs (and some strains even longer).

APPENDIX D - HAIR CARE SUGGESTIONS

HAIR CARE.

A GREAT WAY TO SHAMPOO
Shampooing is the first step in hair care, and is important if you want to achieve healthy looking hair.

GET THE MOST OUT OF YOUR SHAMPOO
- Pour a small amount of shampoo into palms; rub together for a thick lather.
- Massage shampoo gently into hair working downward from forehead, concentrating on hairline around the ears, working towards the back of the neck.
- Rinse thoroughly (water should be lukewarm for dry hair and cool for oily hair to help close pores).

A GREAT WAY TO CONDITION
Now that you're on your way to healthy looking hair, finish with a conditioner designed for your hair type. Conditioning helps restore vitality to hair damaged by the stress of the sun, wind, pollution, electric hair appliances, and other factors such as dieting, smoking and illness. Conditioners need to be combed through before being rinsed out thoroughly.

MY STYLE
A great haircut is basic to any hairstyle. It may be one length or layered. Many times the haircut is the style itself. The key to a great hairstyle is regular cutting – every 6 to 8 weeks.

HAIR CARE HINTS:
- Avoid combs with sharp teeth or rough edges that can irritate the scalp and break hair. Avoid harsh nylon or metal bristle brushes.
- Avoid using rubber bands in your hair; always use coated elastic when you wear your hair back and never put your hair back too tightly.
- To help protect your hair from the harmful effect of chlorine or salt water, apply hair moisturiser to damp hair after a day at the beach.
- Leave for one hour and rinse out.
- Massaging egg yolk and olive oil into your hair is a good hair reviver – don't forget to rinse it out well!
- Take extra care if you have a colour in your hair. Chlorine and salt water can discolour your hair.

APPENDIX E - A TEACUP STORY

A TEA CUP
story

A couple went into an antique shop one day and found a beautiful teacup sitting on a shelf. They took it off the shelf, so they could look at it more closely, and said, "We really want to buy this gorgeous cup."

All of the sudden, the teacup began to talk, saying, "I wasn't always like this. There was a time when I was just a cold, hard, colourless lump of clay. One day my master picked me up and said, 'I could do something with this.' Then he started to pat me, and roll me, and change my shape."

"I said, 'What are you doing? That hurts. I don't know if I want to look like this! Stop!' But he said, 'Not yet.'"

"Then he put me on a wheel and began to spin me around and around and around, until I screamed, 'Let me off, I am getting dizzy!' 'Not yet,' he said."

"Then he shaped me into a cup and put me in a hot oven. I cried, 'Let me out! It's hot in here, I am suffocating.' But he just looked at me through that little glass window and smiled and said, 'Not yet.'"

"When he took me out, I thought his work on me was over, but then he started to paint me. I couldn't believe what he did next. He put me back into the oven, and I said, 'You have to believe me, I can't stand this! Please let me out!' But he said, 'Not yet.'"

"Finally, he took me out of the oven and set me up on a shelf where I thought he had forgotten me. Then one day he took me off the shelf and held me before a mirror. I couldn't believe my eyes, I had become a beautiful teacup that everyone wants to buy."

AUTHOR UNKNOWN

APPENDIX F – I HAVE THE POWER OF CHOICE

STOP.
THINK.
CHOOSE.

We decide how we want to behave. Don't let your **FEELINGS** *decide for you but take your feelings into* **CONSIDERATION** *and use them to your* **ADVANTAGE.**

STOP.
THINK.
CHOOSE.

We decide how we want to behave. Don't let your **FEELINGS** *decide for you but take your feelings into* **CONSIDERATION** *and use them to your* **ADVANTAGE.**

STOP.
THINK.
CHOOSE.

We decide how we want to behave. Don't let your **FEELINGS** *decide for you but take your feelings into* **CONSIDERATION** *and use them to your* **ADVANTAGE.**

STOP.
THINK.
CHOOSE.

We decide how we want to behave. Don't let your **FEELINGS** *decide for you but take your feelings into* **CONSIDERATION** *and use them to your* **ADVANTAGE.**

APPENDIX G - THE RIBBON GAME

THE RIBBON GAME.

RED
Passionate, Bold, Loving, Loyal, Strong

YELLOW
Bright, Happy, Cheerful, Enthusiastic

GREEN
Creative, Unique, Quirky, Interesting, Eclectic

BLUE
Calm, Considerate, Consistent, Patient, Down to earth, Caring, Compassionate, Kind, Sensitive

PURPLE
Influential, Responsible, Dedicated, Courageous, Intelligent

SILVER
Elegant, Graceful, Beautiful, Respectful

WHITE
Honest, Integrity, Humble

APPENDIX H - FINISH THE SENTENCE

FINISH THIS SENTENCE.

If I could do
ANYTHING
I would like to...

_____

_____

The comic
CHARACTER
I would like to be like is...

_____

_____

If I were to
WRITE A BOOK
it would be...

_____

_____

If I were a
A MUSICAL INSTRUMENT
I would be...

_____

_____

APPENDIX H - FINISH THE SENTENCE

FINISH THIS SENTENCE.

My
FAVOURITE MOVIE
of all time is...

_____

_____

What
MAKES ME LAUGH
is...

_____

_____

For alternative icebreakers see Appendix A.

APPENDIX I - SEEDS OF GREATNESS

Seeds of Greatness
"I believe the seeds of greatness are within us all. The key is in creating the correct environment for them to then surface into reality"

Seeds of Greatness
"I believe the seeds of greatness are within us all. The key is in creating the correct environment for them to then surface into reality"

Seeds of Greatness
"I believe the seeds of greatness are within us all. The key is in creating the correct environment for them to then surface into reality"

Seeds of Greatness
"I believe the seeds of greatness are within us all. The key is in creating the correct environment for them to then surface into reality"

Seeds of Greatness
"I believe the seeds of greatness are within us all. The key is in creating the correct environment for them to then surface into reality"

Seeds of Greatness
"I believe the seeds of greatness are within us all. The key is in creating the correct environment for them to then surface into reality"

IMAGINE

BIRTHDAY SPEECHES

Imagine it is your birthday. What would you like people to say about you for your birthday speech? What would you like people to write about you on your birthday card?

LIKES

If you had the total approval and admiration of everyone, regardless of what you do, what would you do with your life?

ROLE MODELS

What role models do you look up to? Who inspires you? What personal strengths or qualities do they have that you admire?

CHARACTER STRENGTHS

What personal strengths and qualities do you already have? Which ones would you like to develop? How would you like to apply them?

WEALTH

Imagine you win the lottery or inherit a fortune. How would you spend it? Who would you share it with?

APPENDIX K - CELEBRATION SAMPLE MENU

PLEASE TICK YOUR SELECTION

desserts

☐ **BON VIVANT (WHEAT FREE)**

The Bon Vivant is a signature creation consisting of two layers; the first a soft flourless hazelnut cake, the top a smooth baked chocolate mousse.

Scrumptious!

☐ **ORANGE ALMOND TORTE (WHEAT & DAIRY FREE)**

A flourless cake, made with oranges and almond meal. Finished with an apricot glaze and a border of flaked almonds.

Delicious...

☐ **BLUEBERRY CHEESECAKE**

Speaks for itself... *Mmmmm...*

drinks

☐ coffee ☐ tea ☐ herbal tea ☐ hot chocolate

EXTRAS

☐ full cream milk ☐ skim milk ☐ no milk ☐ sugar ___ tsp

APPENDIX L - SHINE SCROLL & CERTIFICATE

THIS IS TO CERTIFY THAT...

i have and will always have...

WORTH!

BODY AND SOUL, I AM WONDERFULLY MADE! I AM SOMEBODY!! I HAVE IMMEASURABLE VALUE.

I am unique, matchless and incomparable; no one in the *ENTIRE* world at present or in *ALL* the ages of time has my great gifts, abilities, heart or talents. What a woman I AM... no one has been me and no one will *EVER* be like me. Because *I AM WORTH TAKING CARE OF MYSELF*, I remind myself and the world that *"I AM A MASTERPIECE!"* There is nobody like me and there will never be anyone like me. I can't fit into anybody else's mould. I can't be compared to anyone... not even my sister, mother or friends. My *WORTH* is not related to my performance and what I do – but to my very being. My *WORTH* cannot be earned. It is inborn. I was born with this immeasurable value!!

---

i have and will always have...

STRENGTH!

My strength comes when I use my self-control for good, for myself and for others.
Choosing safe friends, good decision-making (with my mind & not from my feelings) which empowers me to *ACT* and not *REACT*. The quality of my life is a direct result of *MY* choices. Stop. Think. Choose.

---

i have and will always have...

PURPOSE!

MY LIFE COUNTS. I AM UNIQUE! I HAVE PURPOSE.
I am custom made, a masterpiece, one-of-a-kind. I will be the best ME that I can be.
I have to realise that if I'm going to succeed; failing can be a part of the journey...
the important part to remember is to not stay down!

Never a failure, always a lesson.

I will learn from my mistakes and move forward.
It doesn't matter where I've been; It's where I'm going that counts!
I am able to rise above any circumstance and turn it into good!

SHINE FACILITATOR　　　　　　SHINE CO-FACILITATOR　　　　　　DATE

SHINE
CERTIFICATE OF **ACHIEVEMENT** TO RECOGNISE

FOR SUCCESSFULLY COMPLETING **SHINEGIRL**

"i will be the best me that i can be!"

WORTH. STRENGTH. PURPOSE.

APPENDIX M - FEELING CARDS

ANGRY

SHINEGIRL
WORTH. STRENGTH. PURPOSE.

HAPPY

SHINEGIRL
WORTH. STRENGTH. PURPOSE.

SAD

SHINEGIRL
WORTH. STRENGTH. PURPOSE.

FEARFUL

SHINEGIRL
WORTH. STRENGTH. PURPOSE.

COMBINATION

SHINEGIRL
WORTH. STRENGTH. PURPOSE.

APPENDIX M - FEELING CARDS

FURIOUS

IRRITATED

ANNOYED

TICKED OFF

HUMILIATED

APPENDIX M - FEELING CARDS

Frustrated

SHINEGIRL

Hurt

SHINEGIRL

Sarcastic

SHINEGIRL

Disgusted

SHINEGIRL

APPENDIX M - *FEELING CARDS*

EXCITED

SATISFIED

PLEASED

JOYFUL

DELIGHTED

APPENDIX M - FEELING CARDS

COMFORTABLE

HOPEFUL

SURPRISED

POSITIVE

APPENDIX M - FEELING CARDS

GRIEF

MISERABLE

DOWN

DISAPPOINTED

HURT

APPENDIX M - FEELING CARDS

LONELY

FORGOTTEN

REMORSEFUL

REJECTED

APPENDIX M - FEELING CARDS

NERVOUS

TERRIFIED

ANXIOUS

WORRIED

CONCERNED

APPENDIX M - FEELING CARDS

AFRAID

UNCERTAIN

OUT OF CONTROL

UNEASY

APPENDIX M - FEELING CARDS

GUILTY

JEALOUS

SHAME

EMBARRASSED

UNCOMFORTABLE

APPENDIX M - FEELING CARDS

CONFUSED

TORN

ENVIOUS

COMPASSION

APPENDIX N - ADDITIONAL ACTIVITIES

We have included some additional activities for some sessions. These activities are optional and are dependent on whether your target audience would benefit from them.

ACTIVITY: INTRODUCTIONS

Hello everyone! We are proud to introduce to you…
Over the duration of ShineGIRL, each participant will be asked to give a three-minute talk during the sessions.

DISCUSS:
- Some features that define who you are
- A word or phrase that others would describe you as
- Something you believe in
- One thing about yourself that others might find surprising or inspiring!

Most participants will find this exercise challenging, but encourage them to keep going. When we step out of our comfort zone and into something new or different, our confidence increases. This activity encourages the group to begin to think about who they are and how they show their self to the world.

Take into consideration participants who may have high levels of anxiety when it comes to public speaking. Encourage them to do something else to express themselves to the group such as a painting, drawing, or bringing in something that means something to them or explains something about who they are.

This activity is very powerful. Make sure it is incorporated into all sessions so that by the end of the course every girl has participated in this activity.

APPENDIX N - ADDITIONAL ACTIVITIES

etiquette.

NOTE: This suggested activity is not intended to diminish in any way cultural traditions to which a girl may belong. It is designed to equip and empower them to socially interact with all kinds of people in a manner that has grace and dignity.

This section encompasses both giving and receiving respect. We look at good manners, how to conduct oneself in situations, etiquette and how to treat others with courtesy, consideration and generosity.
What is the point of good manners? Why do we need good manners and what good do they do us? Today, in western nations, our lifestyles are much more informal, open and free than the formalities of our parents or grandparents.

Have some discussions on different cultural and generational expectations. What are some of the differences?
Is there any point in having good manners today? Is it just about being a snob? Is it about dos and don'ts? Is it about making you feel all squashed up and hemmed in? (Give an opportunity for individuals in the group to respond.)

The purpose of good manners is to make everyone feel accepted and comfortable. When we are able to express good manners it will help us to acquire self-confidence, self-respect and security. Knowing how to behave in any situation adds to our stature, poise and control. Confidence brings strength. 'Good manners' is the old fashioned term for being respectful of others.

table settings.

CUTLERY: The table setting is laid so that the implements will be used from the outside, in. Working towards the inside, the dessert utensils will be closest to the plate. The diagram on the next page illustrates the place setting and the position of the utensils during the meal and after it is finished.

SERVIETTE: A serviette or napkin is essential and should be placed across the lap before you start to eat (never tucked under the chin unless you're eating ribs!). When the meal is finished, half fold the napkin or scrunch it and place it on the bread plate to your left.

BREAD & BUTTER: A piece of butter should be sliced from the butter disk and placed on the side of the bread plate. From this piece you should butter your roll or bread as you wish. A roll is always broken apart, while bread is always cut.

GLASSWARE: A white wine glass can double as a water glass. It is traditional to serve or at least offer iced water with a meal. Offer to refill water glasses if the waiter doesn't.

APPENDIX N - ADDITIONAL ACTIVITIES

tips for the dinner table.

In Australia, table manners are based on the English style.
An obvious difference is that Americans cut their food and eat with a fork in their right hand. The English style is the fork in the left hand and knife in the right hand.
Be comfortable at the table and maintain posture – sit tall.
Elbows off the table are the general rule.
Bring food up to the mouth instead of hunching over the plate and shovelling in the meal.
Take time, breathe, chew, enjoy. Conversations don't have to be left until after eating. A chat over a lovely meal is a great way to build your confidence (and your friendships!).
When using a soup spoon, move the spoon away to load it, rather than towards the tummy.
We say 'serviettes' and Americans say 'napkins'.

ACTIVITY: SETTING A TABLE

Bring in two dinner settings (can be different styles) with all the extras – serviettes, vase, glasses and so forth. Have them in separate boxes.
Split the group up into two teams and have the two teams set their table.
Use the diagram to the right to see who got most of it right!

NOTES

NOTES

NOTES

NOTES

NOTES

NOTES